Rose Reisman's
LIGHT Vegetarian
COOKING

Rose Reisman's LIGHT Vegetarian COOKING

Robert ROSE

Rose Reisman's Light Vegetarian Cooking

For complete cataloguing data, see page 6.

DESIGN AND PAGE COMPOSITION:	MATTHEWS COMMUNICATIONS DESIGN
PHOTOGRAPHY:	MARK T. SHAPIRO
ART DIRECTION/FOOD PHOTOGRAPHY:	SHARON MATTHEWS
FOOD STYLIST:	KATE BUSH
PROP STYLIST:	MIRIAM GEE
MANAGING EDITOR:	PETER MATTHEWS
INDEXER:	BARBARA SCHON
COLOR SCANS & FILM:	POINTONE GRAPHICS

Cover photo: CARROT ROLL WITH ARTICHOKE GARLIC FILLING *(PAGE 118)*

Distributed in the U.S. by:
Firefly Books (U.S.) Inc.
P.O. Box 1338
Ellicott Station
Buffalo, NY   14205

Distributed in Canada by:
Stoddart Publishing Co. Ltd.
34 Lesmill Road
North York, Ontario
M3B 2T6

ORDER LINES
Tel: (416) 499-8412
Fax: (416) 499-8313

ORDER LINES
Tel: (416) 445-3333
Fax: (416) 445-5967

Published by: Robert Rose Inc. • 156 Duncan Mill Road, Suite 12
Toronto, Ontario, Canada M3B 2N2   Tel: (416) 449-3535

Printed in Canada

1234567 BP 01 00 99 98

CONTENTS

Canadian Cataloguing in Publication Data

Reisman, Rose, 1953–

    Rose Reisman's light vegetarian cooking

Includes index.

ISBN 1-896503-66-7

1. Vegetarian cookery. 2. Low-fat diet – Recipes. I. Title. II. Title Light vegetarian cooking

TX837.R45 1998   641.5'636   C97-932610-9

ACKNOWLEDGEMENTS

To an amazing group of people who virtually do the entire job without me!

Bob Dees, my mentor and friend, whose hard work and diligence has made our company, Robert Rose Inc., a number-one success.

Matthews Communications Design, with particular thanks to Peter and Sharon Matthews, who look after all the editorial, design, art direction and production work on my books.

Mark Shapiro, who performs such magicial work with his camera that I no longer rush him. The results of his extraordinary attention to detail can be seen in the beautiful photos.

Kate Bush, food stylist extraordinaire.

Miriam Gee, for her work in obtaining the props that appear in the photographs.

Lesleigh Landry, my assistant testing chef, for her remarkable professional skills in the kitchen, and for her help in editing the recipes.

Lorraine Fullum-Bouchard, for her informative introduction on vegetarian nutrition.

To Ruby and Lily for their assistance in my home and with the preparation and shopping for literally hundreds of recipes tested.

Denise Amram and Lori Bartholomew at Robert Rose, for their excellent execution of all matters relating to books and products.

Dianne Hargrave, for her ongoing efforts as my publicist.

Stoddart Publishing and Firefly Books; respectively, our distributors in Canada and the U.S.

And finally, no acknowledgements could be complete without mentioning my lifelong buddy, Kathy, who is always there to taste recipes, take home the extras, give me honest opinions, and to join me on walks with my two German shephards to "discuss" my work!

PHOTO PROP CREDITS

The publisher and author wish to express their appreciation to the following suppliers of props used in the food photography appearing in this book:

MAVIS JONES COOKWARE • FRENCH COUNTRY INC. • HOMEFRONT

NESTINGS • ZARRY FINE LINEN / FACTORY DIRECT FRANCE

My love and dedication grows daily
for the inspiration that surrounds me:

My unbelievable husband Sam,
my loving and remarkable children,
Natalie, David, Laura, and Adam
and to Aspen and Meiko,
my faithful and loving German shepherds.

It is my family that gives me my spirit.

Dear Friends and Supporters,

We all know that breast cancer is a serious disease that will affect one in nine women during her lifetime. But progress is being made — in early diagnosis, in treatment, and in understanding the methods of preventing breast cancer.

The National Breast Cancer Fund was established to support this progress with direct financial support for community-based breast cancer prevention, treatment and research programs across Canada. Our primary objective is to ensure that funds are placed where they will have the most immediate benefit — to locally administered facilities dedicated to the care and support of women whose lives have been affected by breast cancer.

The funds raised through the sale of Rose Reisman's cookbooks have been essential to the work of the NBCF. We are both grateful and pleased to be associated with ***Rose Reisman's Light Vegetarian Cooking***.

Our thanks to Rose for her tireless efforts — and to all the people who buy her books. *You* are making a difference.

Sincerely,

Monica Wright-Roberts

President
National Breast Cancer Fund

Dear Friends,

Since its founding in 1978 by the late Mimi Kaplan and Ann Marcou, the Y-ME National Breast Cancer Organization has been offering information and support to breast cancer patients, their families and friends.

It is is our belief that a well-informed patient is better able to cope with her diagnosis. Moreover, we believe it is crucial for women to be full partners with their medical team so that decisions made will reflect the personal needs of that patient. To this end, Y-ME is empowering thousands of women every month through its national hotline and support groups. Y-ME has also been representing women with breast cancer in Washington, D.C., and has successfully lobbied for more research dollars to end this epidemic. Until there is a cure, Y-ME will continue to voice the concerns of the women and men touched by this disease.

Y-ME is delighted to join with Canada's National Breast Cancer Fund in promoting ***Rose Reisman's Light Vegetarian Cooking***. The funds raised through this project will help our organizations meet the ultimate goal — a world without breast cancer.

Sincerely,

Susan M. Nathanson, Ph.D.

Executive Director
Y-ME National Breast Cancer Organization

INTRODUCTION

Rose Reisman cooks light vegetarian? Frankly, if you'd told me a few years ago that I would write this book, I wouldn't have believed you. Like many people, I associated the term "vegetarian" with earnestly bland concoctions of beans, tofu and seaweed. Healthy, yes, but flavorful? Forget it.

Boy, was I ever wrong! Today more and more people are eating vegetarian meals. And they're discovering, as I did in creating the recipes for this book, that vegetarian food can be every bit as delicious as meat-based cuisine. What's more, vegetarianism is no longer an all-or-nothing dietary choice. While some vegetarians consume no animal products whatsoever, others include dairy ingredients and/or eggs. And then there are the "occasional vegetarians" — people who simply choose to include more meatless meals in their diet.

And why not? Certainly there is plenty of evidence that vegetarian food — with its emphasis on fruits, vegetables and grains — can offer a number of important health benefits. Still, it's important to recognize that vegetarianism is not an automatic passport to good health. And that brings me to why I've made this a "light" vegetarian cookbook.

What many people don't realize is that vegetarian food is not necessarily low in fat and calories. In fact, many vegetarians are overweight because they consume large amounts of higher-fat dairy products and still indulge once too often in the junk foods. Remember, a bag of potato chips or a chocolate bar is vegetarian food! That's why I've concentrated on providing a sensible balance of protein and carbohydrates, while reducing the fat, calories and cholesterol in my recipes.

As for myself, I'm one of those "occasional vegetarians" I described earlier — that is, on the days I don't feel like meat, fish or chicken I enjoy these great recipes. But when I want meat, I enjoy moderate portions. In fact, one day, after months of testing for this book, my husband finally said, "this recipe would be great with some chicken or fish!" I agreed, and added some. So there you are — be flexible. I believe that this is the answer to any lifetime diet. Eat everything in moderation.

My definition of "vegetarian" for this book includes milk, cheese and eggs, but no fish, meat or chicken products. And within this definition I've come up with 150 deliciously low-fat recipes. I could have kept going; the ideas were endless. Testing these recipes was an apprehensive yet exciting time for family, friends and colleagues. Would they be as successful as those recipes with meat in them? The answer, I think, is a resounding YES! In fact, I believe these vegetarian dishes are tastier and more interesting because, without the addition of meat, I've had to be that much more creative. I had a blast, and I am absolutely thrilled with the results.

Canada's Food Guide to Healthy Eating suggests we consume 5 to 12 servings daily of grains, 5 to 10 servings of fruits and vegetables, and keep fats to a minimum. Well, the recipes in *Light Vegetarian Cooking* definitely adhere to this prescription. Here you'll find tantalizing appetizers such as **Caesar Tortilla Pizzas** and my **Hot Three-Cheese Dill Artichoke Bake**. Tasty, exciting soups, include **Wild Mushroom and Barley Soup**, **Roasted Tomato and Corn Soup** and **Sweet Potato Orange Soup** — all featuring delicious vegetables and fresh seasonings.

My salads use just about every vegetable under the sun, accented with flavorful cheeses and dressings that are low in fat and incorporate a wide variety of international flavors. How about **Tomato, Artichoke and Potato Salad with Oriental Dressing** or **Split-Pea and Rice Greek Salad** or **Asian Tabbouleh Salad**?

Try my vegetarian main or side dishes — they're so creative and delicious that you'll never miss meat, fish or chicken! These include dishes like **Portobello Mushroom Sandwiches**, **Carrot Roll with Artichoke Garlic Filling** and **Potato Crust Pesto Pizza**. They're honestly *so good*, you'll have a hard time restricting yourself to just one portion. But then, they're low in fat — so don't worry if you can't resist an extra helping.

In the pasta and grains section of this book, you'll discover that there's more to this category of food than brown rice and lentils. Just try recipes such as **Bean and Sweet Potato Chili on Garlic Polenta** or **Barley Cabbage Rolls in Tomato Basil Sauce** or **Orzo Spinach Mushroom Pie**.

And let's not forget my favorite section — desserts! Indulge in fantastic lower-fat recipes such as **Sour Cream Brownie Cheesecake**, **Banana Chocolate Chip Cake** and **Pear and Raisin Custard Crumble**.

As always, my recipes are quick and easy to prepare, with ingredients that are readily available at your local supermarket. All meals are nutritionally analyzed and provide informative tips and make-ahead suggestions. And, as in the past, I continue the fight against breast cancer, with a portion of the proceeds from the sale of this book going to the National Breast Cancer Fund in Canada and Y-ME in the U.S. In fact, thanks to all the people who have purchased my previous books, and through the personal efforts of my husband and myself, over $1,000,000 has been raised for this cause. That's the kind of difference each of us can make when we work together. But more is always needed. So please continue supporting the fight against breast cancer.

For Canadian readers, you can now find me on the Life Network, where I host my own show, "Free for the Asking." Tune in for a lively discussion of food, nutrition, fitness and general good health. There are great guests and wonderful information.

Finally, I've joined the wired world of e-mail. Send me your comments and suggestions at *aspen@astral.magic.ca* — I would love to hear from you.

So here's my version of light vegetarian cooking. I hope it opens a new world of cuisine for you and your family. Enjoy!

Rose Reisman

NUTRITIONAL ADVICE

These days more and more people are adopting a vegetarian diet — if not exclusively, then at least for a growing number of meals throughout the week. Just take a look at what's on the shelves of your local supermarket: various types of tofu and other soy-based products (including "veggie" burgers and hot dogs), prepared hummus, bean salads, plus a wide variety of canned or bottled legumes. These and many other vegetarian foods, once found only in health food stores, are now mainstream products.

While there is no single reason for the growth of vegetarianism in the late 1990s, health concerns are clearly an important factor. Research has provided evidence that elements of a vegetarian diet — notably grains, legumes, fresh fruits and vegetables — can help to improve overall health and reduce the incidence of cardiovascular disease, as well as certain types of cancer.

As acceptance of vegetarianism has increased, so has the number of different types of vegetarian. At one extreme are vegans (pronounced (VEE-guns), who consume only plant-based food and strictly avoid anything of animal origin, often including derivative products such as gelatin or even honey. Typically, this diet reflects a lifestyle that excludes all animal products, such as leather, silk, wool, goose down or tallow soap.

Occupying the other end of the vegetarian spectrum are what Rose describes in her Introduction as "occasional vegetarians" — those people who are cutting down on meat (particularly red meat) dishes, and are replacing them with vegetarian alternatives. The middle ground is occupied by people who have given up meat but may include milk and other dairy products (lacto-vegetarians), eggs (ovo vegetarians) or both (lacto-ovo-vegetarians). The latter definition is most typical of those North Americans who describe themselves as "vegetarians."

Depending on what type of vegetarian you are, there are a number of dietary issues that should be addressed to ensure that you enjoy balanced and complete nutrition. For example, if you give up meat, you will need to choose vegetarian alternatives that are comparably high in protein, as well as essential minerals such as iron and zinc. Similarly, foregoing milk products means that you will need to find another good source for the calcium your body requires.

A vegetarian diet, like any other, requires careful planning to ensure an adequate supply of nutrients to promote optimal health – that is, the nutrients your body needs to build new cells, repair tissue, supply energy and regulate bodily functions. The key here is to have a balanced diet — one that consists of selections from each of the four food groups, including grains, fruits, vegetables, legumes, nuts and seeds.

MAKING SENSIBLE CHOICES

To assist you with your food choices, use your federal Canadian or U.S government food guide (available from most nutritionists or health department offices) and/or the Adult Vegetarian Food Chart shown on the opposite page.

The vegetarian food chart was developed from *Canada's Food Guide to Healthy Eating* and will be particularly useful to vegans and ovo-vegetarians who, without the nutrients provided by meat, poultry, fish, milk and dairy products, face a particular challenge in balancing their diet — specifically, in obtaining sufficient quantities of calcium, vitamin B-12, vitamin D, iron, zinc and omega-3 fatty acids.

In planning your daily meals, refer to the recommended number of daily servings for each food group. Choose the appropriate number of servings from those food groups specific to your type of vegetarian diet and level of activity.

A basic framework when planning meals is to start with grains (such as whole-grain pasta and breads, rice, millet, couscous and barley). You will need a minimum of 5 servings per day. Next, choose the vegetables (in season, if possible): Choose one leafy green vegetable, one colored vegetable (red, deep orange or yellow) and one other vegetable for variety. Enjoy a minimum of 3 servings each day. Next, select a minimum 2 servings of fruit — again, in season, if possible — with one of these being colored red, orange or yellow.

Next choose legumes such as beans, lentils and peas, legume derivatives such as tofu or tempeh, or nuts and seeds for protein; if your dietary choice allows, other possible selections from this category include eggs, chicken or fish. You will need 2 to 3 servings a day.

Milk products (or milk alternatives) should be selected next to meet your calcium needs. Choose a minimum of 2 to 4 daily servings of milk products or 6 servings of milk alternatives.

Now review your choices and draft your shopping list. Remember to focus desserts on fresh fruit and snacks on grains, fruits, vegetables and/or calcium-rich foods.

Finally, keep in mind that while specific items within each food group have similar nutritive properties, they are not identical. For example, oranges are rich in vitamin C, apples are not; broccoli is an excellent source of beta-carotene, potatoes are not. That's why it's important to eat a wide variety of foods *within* each food group on a weekly basis.

AVOIDING THE PITFALLS

Many people believe that switching to a vegetarian diet is simply a matter of replacing meat (and/or milk, cheese, etc.) with more of the same vegetables that would normally accompany it. This is just one common mistake that can lead to poor nutrition. Let's look at some of these pitfalls in detail:

• **Replacing meat with more vegetables, rice or pasta.** If you're not going to eat meat, then you'll need to replace it with a high-quality vegetable protein, such as that found in cooked legumes, tofu, tem-

ADULT VEGETARIAN FOOD CHART

GRAIN PRODUCTS

5 to 12 servings a day. *Whole-grain products are recommended.*

Bread	1 slice (25 g)	Chapati or roti	1 (25 to 40 g)	Pita bread, 6-inch (15 cm) size	Half (25 g)
Bagel, small	Half (25 g)	Crackers	2 to 6 (25 g)	Popcorn, popped	3 cups (750 mL)
Bannock	1 oz (25 g)	Hamburger or hot dog bun	Half (25 to 40 g)	Rice or corn cakes	2 to 3 (25 g)
Cereal, ready-to-eat, dry	1 oz (25 g)	Muffin, small	1 (40 g)	Roll, small	1 (25 to 40 g)
Cereal, cooked	3/4 cup (175 mL)	Pancake or waffle, small	1 (40 g)	Tortilla, flour	1 (25 g)
Cooked grains, such as bulgur, couscous, millet or rice	1/2 cup (125 mL)	Pasta, cooked	1/2 cup (125 mL)	Wheat germ	2 tbsp (25 mL)

VEGETABLES AND FRUITS

5 to 10 servings a day. *Include 1 to 2 servings of dark green leafy vegetables (kale, collard, bok choy, Chinese cabbage, okra or broccoli) and 1 or more other vegetables each day. Include 2 to 3 fruits daily. Choose 1 fruit or 1 vegetable serving high in vitamin C, such as citrus fruit, kiwi, all berries, fortified fruit juices, guava, papaya, broccoli, brussels sprouts, cauliflower, collard or snow peas.*

Vegetable or fruit, fresh, frozen or canned	1/2 cup (125 mL)	Apricot, kiwi, clementine, plum or other small fruit	2	Apple, banana, orange or peach	1
Vegetable or fruit juice	1/2 cup (125 mL)	Potato, carrot or tomato, medium size	1	Salad or fresh strawberries	1 cup (250 mL)

BEANS AND BEAN ALTERNATIVES

2 to 4 servings a day. *To increase iron absorption from these foods, eat a vegetable or fruit high in vitamin C at the same meal. (See section above for suggestions.)*

Cooked legumes; see section below for examples	1/2 to 1 cup (125 to 250 mL)	Egg, medium	1 to 2	Nuts and seeds	3 to 4 tbsp (45 to 60 mL)
Nut or seed butter, such as peanut butter	2 to 3 tbsp (25 to 45 mL)	Tofu or tempeh, (about 3 oz [75 g])	1/3 cup (75 mL)	Meat analogs, such as tofu burgers	1 patty (70 to 80 g)
		Soy milk	1 cup (250 mL)		

MILK AND MILK ALTERNATIVES

4 to 6 servings a day. *Soy and rice milk are now available fortified with calcium and/or vitamin D. Check labels to compare the amounts of these nutrients offered by different brands.*

Cheddar cheese	1 oz (25 g)	Legumes, cooked, such as pinto, butter or kidney beans, or chickpeas	1 1/2 cups (375 mL)	Greens, raw, such as broccoli, bok choy, collards, kale, okra, and Chinese cabbage	2 cups (500 mL)
Milk or yogurt	1/2 cup (125 mL)				
Tofu set with calcium	1/4 cup (50 mL)	Legumes, cooked, such as soybeans, white beans, navy, great northern and black beans	1 cup (250 mL)	Greens, cooked, (see previous)	1 cup (250 mL)
Blackstrap molasses	1 tbsp (15 mL)			Canned salmon, with bones	1/2 cup (125 mL)
Almonds	1/3 cup (75 mL)				
Sesame tahini	2 tbsp (25 mL)	Figs, dried	5 (100 g)		

peh, meat analogs (such as tofu burgers and wieners) or nuts and seeds. Vegetables and grains alone will not deliver the protein you need. In this book, Rose has created many wonderful soups, salads and casseroles that provide tasty combinations of beans and lentils. Try a few. One of my favorites is CURRIED COUSCOUS WITH TOMATOES AND CHICKPEAS (page 145). Wondering what to do with tofu? Try the HOISIN STIR-FRIED VEGETABLES AND TOFU OVER RICE NOODLES. Delicious!

• **Replacing meat with cheese.** Yes, cheese is a source of protein. But unlike meat and legumes, it lacks iron and is almost completely devoid of zinc. Also, if you choose a regular variety of cheese, you could end up adding a lot of unwanted fat and calories to your diet. Use some of Rose's recipes to explore ingredients such as tofu, beans, peas and lentils.

• **Substituting unfortified soy or rice beverages for milk.** While soy and rice beverages have been fortified with added calcium and vitamin D in the U.S. for many years, this has been allowed only recently in Canada. Without fortification, soy and rice beverages are a poor substitute for milk, so be sure to check the labels of different brands carefully.

GETTING THE NUTRIENTS YOU NEED

Iron. It is important for vegetarians to choose iron-rich foods and to ensure that the iron is well absorbed. Important sources of iron include legumes, grains and cereals, as well as vegetables such as broccoli, bok choy and green peas. (Contrary to popular belief, spinach and rhubarb are not good sources of iron; the oxalates in these foods bind the iron, making it largely unavailable, even after cooking.) Keep in mind, too, that iron derived from plant food (called "non-heme" iron) is absorbed quite differently from the "heme" iron found in meat. To enhance absorption, eat iron-rich vegetarian fare in combination with foods containing plenty of vitamin C. Cooking in an iron pan also increases the amount of iron in your diet. Try to avoid tea (or other high-tannin beverages) at mealtimes, as this impairs iron absorption.

Zinc. This is an important mineral in which vegetarians are often deficient (as are many non-vegetarians). Good sources of zinc include nuts (almonds, cashews and walnuts), seeds (sesame, flax and sunflower), legumes (black, lima, mung, garbanzo and pinto beans), whole grains (millet and wheat germ), vegetables (peas and potatoes with skins), as well as avocados, nutritional yeast and, if your diet allows, eggs.

Vitamin B-12. This nutrient is also a challenge — particularly for vegans, who should have their blood levels of vitamin B-12 levels checked annually. Milk and eggs are good sources of this vitamin; otherwise, you may need to rely on vitamin supplements or certain types of nutritional yeast which can be sprinkled on salads, cooked grains or casseroles.

Vitamin D. This vitamin can be obtained from milk, fortified margarine or supplements. Exposure to sunlight is another source — 10 to 30 minutes a day, depending on weather conditions and skin type.

Omega-3 fatty acids. To maintain necessary levels of this nutrient, consume 1/2 tsp (2 mL) flax seed oil or 1 tbsp (15 mL) canola oil or 3 tbsp (45 mL) walnuts or pumpkin seeds.

Enjoy vegetarian good health!

Lorraine Fullum-Bouchard, B.Sc., RD

APPETIZERS

Sautéed Potato Pesto Pita Pizzas

◆▪◆▪◆▪◆◀━━━▶◆▪◆▪◆▪◆

TIP

To soften sun-dried tomatoes, cover with boiling water and let soak 15 minutes; drain and chop.

Use 3 small 6-inch (15 cm) flour tortillas instead of pita bread.

Keep grated potatoes in cold water to prevent browning.

Pesto sauce can be kept frozen until ready to use.

For a stronger flavor, use 2 oz (50 g) feta or goat cheese instead of mozzarella.

MAKE AHEAD

Prepare mixture up to 1 day in advance. Bake just before serving.

PER SERVING (6)	
Calories	299
Protein	9 g
Fat, total	10 g
Fat, saturated	2.5 g
Carbohydrates	44 g
Sodium	217 mg
Cholesterol	7 mg
Fiber	3 g

Preheat oven to 400° F (200° C)
Baking sheet sprayed with vegetable spray

2 tsp	vegetable oil	10 mL
1 cup	chopped red onions	250 mL
2 tsp	minced garlic	10 mL
1/2 tsp	dried oregano	2 mL
8 oz	potatoes, peeled and shredded (about 2)	250 g
	Freshly ground black pepper to taste	
3	6-inch (15 cm) pita breads	3
1/4 cup	pesto (see recipe, page 68)	50 mL
1/3 cup	chopped softened sun-dried tomatoes (see Tip, at left)	75 mL
1/4 cup	sliced black olives	50 mL
1/2 cup	shredded part-skim mozzarella cheese (about 2 oz [50 g])	125 mL

1. In a large nonstick frying pan sprayed with vegetable spray, heat oil over medium-high heat. Add onions, garlic and oregano; cook 5 minutes or until onions are softened. Stir in potatoes; cook, stirring often and scraping bottom of pan, until potatoes are browned and tender, about 25 to 30 minutes. Season to taste with pepper. Remove from heat.

2. Spread each pita with pesto and place on baking sheet. Divide potato mixture evenly among pitas. Sprinkle sun-dried tomatoes and black olives evenly over pitas; top with mozzarella.

3. Bake 10 minutes, or until cheese is melted.

Caesar Tortilla Pizzas

TIP

I tried this pizza at the Planet Hollywood restaurant in Manhattan; this low-fat version is, I think, even more delicious than the original.

Try using pita bread instead of tortillas.

MAKE AHEAD

Prepare pizzas early in day and bake just before serving.

PER SERVING (4)	
Calories	317
Protein	14 g
Fat, total	13 g
Fat, saturated	4.0 g
Carbohydrates	38 g
Sodium	408 mg
Cholesterol	69 mg
Fiber	1 g

Preheat oven to 400° F (200° C)
Baking sheet

Sauce

1	egg yolk	1
2 tbsp	grated Parmesan cheese	25 mL
2 tsp	freshly squeezed lemon juice	10 mL
1 tsp	minced garlic	5 mL
1/2 tsp	Dijon mustard	2 mL
2 tbsp	olive oil	25 mL
4	small flour tortillas (6-inch [15 cm]) or 2 large (10-inch [25 cm])	4

Toppings

1 cup	diced seeded plum tomatoes	250 mL
3/4 cup	shredded part-skim mozzarella cheese (about 3 oz [75 g])	175 mL
2 tbsp	grated Parmesan cheese	25 mL
1/2 cup	chopped romaine lettuce	125 mL

1. In a small bowl, whisk together egg yolk, 2 tbsp (25 mL) Parmesan cheese, lemon juice, garlic and mustard. Gradually add olive oil, whisking constantly. Put tortillas on baking sheet and divide sauce among tortillas, spreading to the edges.

2. Divide tomatoes, mozzarella and remaining Parmesan among tortillas.

3. Bake 12 to 14 minutes or until cheese melts and tortillas start to brown. Top with lettuce, slice and serve immediately.

Bean and Cheese Tortilla Slices

1 cup	canned red kidney beans, rinsed and drained	250 mL
1 tbsp	freshly squeezed lemon juice	15 mL
1/2 tsp	chili powder	2 mL
1/2 tsp	minced garlic	2 mL
3/4 cup	5% smooth ricotta cheese	175 mL
3 tbsp	chopped green onions	45 mL
3 tbsp	chopped fresh coriander	45 mL
2 tbsp	light sour cream	25 mL
1 tbsp	light mayonnaise	15 mL
4	small 6-inch (15 cm) flour tortillas	4

1. In a food processor or with a fork in a bowl, mash together beans, lemon juice, chili powder and garlic. In a separate bowl, combine ricotta, green onions, coriander, sour cream and mayonnaise; stir until well mixed.

2. Divide ricotta mixture among tortillas and spread over surface. Top with bean mixture. Roll tightly, cover and chill 30 minutes.

3. Cut each roll into 6 pieces and serve.

PER SERVING (6)	
Calories	132
Protein	9 g
Fat, total	3 g
Fat, saturated	2.0 g
Carbohydrates	17 g
Sodium	208 mg
Cholesterol	9 mg
Fiber	3 g

Brie-Stuffed Mushrooms

TIP

Don't throw out those mushroom stems — use them in salads or soups, or sauté in a nonstick skillet and serve as a side vegetable dish.

Roast your own red bell peppers or buy water-packed roasted red peppers.

Use another soft cheese of your choice to replace the Brie.

MAKE AHEAD

Fill mushroom caps up to 1 day in advance. Bake just before serving.

Preheat oven to 400° F (200° C)

Baking sheet

16 to 20	medium mushrooms	16 to 20
2 oz	Brie cheese	50 g
1/4 cup	chopped roasted red peppers	50 mL
1/4 cup	chopped green onions	50 mL
3 tbsp	dried bread crumbs	45 mL
1 tsp	minced garlic	5 mL
1/2 tsp	dried basil	2 mL

1. Wipe mushrooms; remove stems and reserve for another use. (See Tip, at left.) Place on baking sheet.

2. In a small bowl, stir together Brie, red peppers, green onions, bread crumbs, garlic and basil. Divide mixture among mushroom caps, approximately 1 1/2 tsp (7 mL) per cap.

3. Bake 15 minutes, or until mushrooms release their liquid. Serve warm or at room temperature.

PER SERVING

Calories	86
Protein	5 g
Fat, total	4 g
Fat, saturated	2.0 g
Carbohydrates	9 g
Sodium	205 mg
Cholesterol	13 mg
Fiber	1 g

Hot Three-Cheese Dill Artichoke Bake

TIP

This tastes like the traditional hot artichoke dip loaded with fat and calories, but has less than half the fat.

Serve over French bread or with vegetables.

MAKE AHEAD

Prepare up to 1 day in advance. Bake just before serving.

Preheat oven to 350° F (180° C)
Small casserole dish

1	can (14 oz [398 mL]) artichoke hearts, drained and halved	1
1/2 cup	shredded part-skim mozzarella cheese (about 2 oz [50 g])	125 mL
1/3 cup	shredded Swiss cheese (about 1 1/2 oz [35 g])	75 mL
1/3 cup	minced fresh dill (or 1 tsp [5 mL] dried)	75 mL
1/4 cup	light sour cream	50 mL
3 tbsp	light mayonnaise	45 mL
1 tbsp	freshly squeezed lemon juice	15 mL
1 tsp	minced garlic	5 mL
Pinch	cayenne pepper	Pinch
1 tbsp	grated Parmesan cheese	15 mL

1. In a food processor, combine artichoke hearts, mozzarella and Swiss cheeses, dill, sour cream, mayonnaise, lemon juice, garlic and cayenne. Process on and off just until combined but still chunky. Place in a small casserole dish. Sprinkle with Parmesan cheese.

2. Bake uncovered 10 minutes. Broil 3 to 5 minutes just until top is slightly browned. Serve warm with crackers.

PER SERVING (8)	
Calories	79
Protein	5 g
Fat, total	5 g
Fat, saturated	2.0 g
Carbohydrates	6 g
Sodium	271 mg
Cholesterol	10 mg
Fiber	2 g

Creamy Sun-Dried Tomato Dip

TIP

To toast pine nuts, bake in 350° F (180° C) oven 8 to 10 minutes or until golden and fragrant. Or, in a non-stick skillet over high heat, toast until browned, about 2 to 3 minutes.

Avoid sun-dried tomatoes packed in oil; these have a lot of extra calories and fat.

Great as a topping with crackers, baguettes or as a dip for vegetables or baked tortilla chips.

Use as a topping for cooked vegetables or on non-vegetarian days for fish or chicken.

MAKE AHEAD

Prepare up to 3 days in advance.

PER SERVING

Calories	113
Protein	7 g
Fat, total	6 g
Fat, saturated	2.0 g
Carbohydrates	10 g
Sodium	413 mg
Cholesterol	7 mg
Fiber	3 g

4 oz	dry-packed sun-dried tomatoes	125 g
3/4 cup	5% ricotta cheese	175 mL
1/2 cup	chopped fresh parsley	125 mL
1/3 cup	BASIC VEGETABLE STOCK (see recipe, page 36) *or* water	75 mL
3 tbsp	chopped black olives	45 mL
2 tbsp	olive oil	25 mL
2 tbsp	toasted pine nuts	25 mL
2 tbsp	grated Parmesan cheese	25 mL
1 tsp	minced garlic	5 mL

1. In a small bowl, pour boiling water to cover over sun-dried tomatoes. Let stand 15 minutes. Drain and chop.

2. In a food processor combine sun-dried tomatoes, ricotta, parsley, stock, olives, olive oil, pine nuts, Parmesan and garlic; process until well combined but still chunky. Makes 1 3/4 cups (425 mL).

Eggplant, Tomato and Fennel Appetizer

TIP

Serve with crackers, or as bruschetta on top of toasted baguette slices.

For an interesting salad, omit Step 2, then serve chilled on top of green beans.

Try over hot pasta.

MAKE AHEAD

Prepare up to 2 days in advance.

2 tsp	vegetable oil	10 mL
2 tsp	minced garlic	10 mL
1 cup	chopped fennel	250 mL
1 cup	chopped onions	250 mL
1 cup	chopped red bell peppers	250 mL
3 cups	diced unpeeled eggplant	750 mL
2 cups	chopped plum tomatoes	500 mL
1/4 cup	sliced green olives	50 mL
1 1/2 tbsp	balsamic vinegar	22 mL
4 tsp	drained capers	20 mL
2 tsp	dried basil	10 mL

1. In a nonstick saucepan, heat oil over medium-high heat. Add garlic, fennel, onions and red peppers; cook, stirring occasionally, 4 minutes. Add eggplant; cook 5 minutes longer, stirring occasionally. Stir in tomatoes, olives, vinegar, capers and basil; reduce heat to medium-low and simmer 15 minutes.

2. Transfer to a food processor; pulse on and off until chunky. Chill.

PER SERVING

Calories	69
Protein	2 g
Fat, total	3 g
Fat, saturated	0.3 g
Carbohydrates	11 g
Sodium	529 mg
Cholesterol	0 mg
Fiber	4 g

Marinated Greek Mushrooms

TIP

The longer the mushrooms marinate, the more flavorful they will be.

If you can't find small button mushrooms, use larger mushrooms and cut into quarters.

To make this a vegan dish, just eliminate the cheese.

MAKE AHEAD

Prepare 1 day in advance. Stir before serving.

1 lb	button mushrooms, cleaned	500 g
1/2 cup	chopped fresh coriander	125 mL
1/2 cup	chopped red onions	125 mL
1/3 cup	sliced black olives	75 mL
1/3 cup	balsamic vinegar	75 mL
2 tbsp	water	25 mL
2 tbsp	olive oil	25 mL
1 tbsp	freshly squeezed lemon juice	15 mL
1 tsp	minced garlic	5 mL
1/2 to 3/4 tsp	chili powder *or* 1/2 tsp (2 mL) minced fresh jalapeno pepper	2 to 4 mL
1/4 tsp	freshly ground black pepper	1 mL
2 oz	feta cheese, crumbled	50 g

1. In a large bowl, stir together mushrooms, coriander, red onions, olives, vinegar, water, olive oil, lemon juice, garlic, chili powder, pepper and feta.

2. Cover and chill 1 hour or overnight, mixing occasionally.

PER SERVING (8)

Calories	71
Protein	2 g
Fat, total	5 g
Fat, saturated	2.0 g
Carbohydrates	5 g
Sodium	125 mg
Cholesterol	6 mg
Fiber	1 g

Mushroom Egg Rolls with Honey Dijon Sauce

MAKES 12

TIP

These delicious low-fat egg rolls are baked rather than deep-fried.

MAKE AHEAD

Prepare rolls up to 1 day in advance. Keep refrigerated.

Preheat oven to 425° F (220° C)
Baking sheet sprayed with vegetable spray

2 tsp	vegetable oil	10 mL
2 tsp	minced garlic	10 mL
1 cup	chopped onions	250 mL
1 cup	chopped red bell peppers	250 mL
1 lb	mushrooms, chopped	500 g
1/4 cup	chopped fresh dill (or 1 tsp [5 mL] dried)	50 mL
1/4 cup	chopped black olives	50 mL
2 tbsp	grated Parmesan cheese	25 mL
2 tsp	drained capers	10 mL
2 oz	feta cheese, crumbled	50 g
12	large (5 1/2-inch [13.5 cm] square) egg roll wrappers	12

Sauce

3 tbsp	light sour cream	45 mL
2 tbsp	light mayonnaise	25 mL
1 tsp	honey	5 mL
1 tsp	Dijon mustard	5 mL

1. In a saucepan heat oil over medium heat. Add garlic, onions and red peppers; cook, covered, 5 minutes or until tender. Transfer to a bowl; set aside.

2. In a large nonstick skillet sprayed with vegetable spray, cook mushrooms over high heat 5 to 8 minutes or until browned and liquid absorbed. Stir into onion mixture, along with dill, olives, Parmesan, capers and feta cheese.

PER SERVING

Calories	124
Protein	5 g
Fat, total	4 g
Fat, saturated	1.0 g
Carbohydrates	19 g
Sodium	329 mg
Cholesterol	7 mg
Fiber	2 g

3. Place 1 egg roll wrapper on work surface with a corner pointing towards you. (Cover the others with a cloth to prevent drying.) Brush edges with water. Put 1/4 cup (50 mL) filling in center. Fold the lower corner up over the filling, fold the 2 side corners in over the filling, and roll the bundle away from you. Transfer to baking sheet. Repeat with remaining filling and wrappers.

4. Bake 15 to 20 minutes, turning at the halfway point, or until golden.

5. Meanwhile, prepare the sauce: In a small bowl, stir together sour cream, mayonnaise, honey and Dijon. Serve as a dipping sauce with the egg rolls.

Mushroom Sun-Dried Tomato Cheese Pâté

◆■◆■◆■◆■◆▶━━◀◆■◆■◆■◆■◆

SERVES 8 TO 10

TIP

Instead of a loaf pan, you can also pour this into a decorative serving dish.

To soften sun-dried tomatoes, cover with boiling water and let soak 15 minutes; drain and chop.

Try wild mushrooms, if available. Oyster mushrooms are a good choice.

MAKE AHEAD

Prepare up to 2 days in advance.

PER SERVING (10)	
Calories	121
Protein	8 g
Fat, total	8 g
Fat, saturated	5.0 g
Carbohydrates	6 g
Sodium	212 mg
Cholesterol	25 mg
Fiber	1 g

9- by 5-inch (2 L) loaf pan lined with plastic wrap

1 1/2 tsp	vegetable oil	7 mL
1/3 cup	chopped onions	75 mL
1 cup	chopped mushrooms	250 mL
1/3 cup	finely chopped red bell peppers	75 mL
1 1/2 cups	5% ricotta cheese	375 mL
1/2 cup	light cream cheese, softened	125 mL
1/3 cup	light sour cream	75 mL
1/3 cup	chopped softened sun-dried tomatoes (see Tip, at left)	75 mL
1/3 cup	chopped fresh dill (or 1 1/2 tsp [7 mL] dried)	75 mL
2 tbsp	freshly squeezed lemon juice	25 mL
2 tbsp	grated Parmesan cheese	25 mL
1 tsp	minced garlic	5 mL
1/4 tsp	freshly ground black pepper	1 mL

1. In a nonstick frying pan, heat oil over medium-high heat. Add onions; cook 4 minutes or until softened. Stir in mushrooms and red peppers; cook 4 minutes longer or until vegetables are tender. Remove from heat.

2. In a large bowl, combine ricotta, cream cheese, sour cream, sun-dried tomatoes, dill, lemon juice, Parmesan, garlic and pepper until well mixed. Stir in cooked vegetables. Pour into prepared loaf pan; refrigerate at least 1 hour. Invert onto a serving platter; peel off plastic wrap. Serve with crackers or bread.

Phyllo Vegetable Purses

MAKES 24

TIPS

Keep phyllo covered so it doesn't dry out and become brittle.

Do not crowd purses on baking sheet, or they may burst as they bake.

These are decorative and look difficult to make, but are very simple.

Soften sun-dried tomatoes by pouring boiling water over top. Let soak 15 minutes, drain and chop.

Roast your own red bell peppers or buy water-packed roasted red peppers.

MAKE AHEAD

Once assembled, purses can be covered and refrigerated until you're ready to bake them.

Prepare purses up to 1 day in advance. Or freeze up to 6 weeks and bake from frozen.

PER SERVING

Calories	111
Protein	4 g
Fat, total	4 g
Fat, saturated	2.0 g
Carbohydrates	13 g
Sodium	246 mg
Cholesterol	8 mg
Fiber	1 g

Preheat oven to 400° F (200° C)
Baking sheets sprayed with vegetable spray

2 tsp	vegetable oil	10 mL
3/4 cup	chopped leeks	175 mL
1/2 cup	finely chopped carrots	125 mL
2 tsp	minced garlic	10 mL
1/2 cup	chopped mushrooms	125 mL
1/3 cup	light cream cheese	75 mL
1/2 cup	chopped fresh coriander	125 mL
1/2 cup	chopped roasted red peppers	125 mL
1/4 cup	chopped softened sun-dried tomatoes (see Tip, at left)	50 mL
3 tbsp	grated Parmesan cheese	45 mL
4	sheets phyllo pastry	4
2 tsp	melted margarine or butter	10 mL

1. In a nonstick saucepan sprayed with vegetable spray, heat oil over medium-low heat. Add leeks, carrots and garlic; cook 5 minutes or until carrots are softened. Stir in mushrooms; cook, stirring, 3 minutes. Remove from heat. Stir in cream cheese until cheese melts. Stir in coriander, roasted peppers, sun-dried tomatoes and Parmesan cheese.

2. Layer 2 sheets of phyllo on a work surface; brush sparingly with melted margarine. With a sharp knife, cut into quarters along long end and cut into thirds along short end, to produce 12 squares. Put approximately 2 tsp (10 mL) filling into center of each square, bring up four corners and pinch in above filling. Transfer to a baking sheet. Repeat with remaining phyllo and filling. Brush tops with any remaining margarine.

3. Bake 8 to 10 minutes or until golden.

Spinach Cheese Squares in Puff Pastry

PER SERVING	
Calories	253
Protein	8 g
Fat, total	17 g
Fat, saturated	4.0 g
Carbohydrates	18 g
Sodium	335 mg
Cholesterol	47 mg
Fiber	1 g

Preheat oven to 400° F (200° C)
Baking sheet sprayed with vegetable spray

1 tsp	margarine *or* butter	5 mL
1/2 cup	chopped onions	125 mL
1 tsp	minced garlic	5 mL
3/4 tsp	dried basil	4 mL
1/2 tsp	dried oregano	2 mL
1/3 cup	frozen chopped spinach, thawed and drained	75 mL
1	egg	1
1/2 cup	5% ricotta cheese	125 mL
1/4 cup	shredded Swiss cheese (about 1 oz [25 g])	50 mL
1 tbsp	grated Parmesan cheese	15 mL
1/4 tsp	freshly ground black pepper	1 mL
7 oz	frozen puff pastry, thawed (half package [14 oz /411 g] frozen puff pastry)	210 g

1. In a nonstick saucepan, melt margarine over medium heat. Add onions, garlic, basil and oregano; cook 4 minutes or until softened. Stir in spinach; cook 2 minutes. Remove from heat; cool slightly.

2. In a bowl stir together egg, ricotta, Swiss, Parmesan and pepper; stir in spinach mixture.

3. On a lightly floured surface, roll puff pastry to an 11-inch (27.5 cm) square. Transfer to baking sheet; tuck ends under to form a ridge on all sides. Spread evenly with spinach mixture.

4. Bake 20 to 25 minutes or until golden. Cut into 16 squares. Serve warm or at room temperature.

Sweet Potato and Maple Syrup Quesadillas

TIP

Instead of large tortillas, you can use about 8 of the small 6-inch (15 cm) size.

Coriander can be replaced with dill, parsley or fresh basil.

Goat cheese can also be replaced with feta, or a milder cheese.

MAKE AHEAD

Prepare potato mixture up to 1 day in advance.

Preheat oven to 425° F (220° C)
Large baking sheet

1 lb	sweet potatoes, peeled and diced	500 g
2 tbsp	maple syrup	25 mL
1/4 tsp	cinnamon	1 mL
1 tsp	vegetable oil	5 mL
1 tsp	minced garlic	5 mL
1/2 cup	chopped green onions	125 mL
1/4 cup	chopped fresh coriander	50 mL
6	large flour tortillas (10-inch [25 cm] size)	6
2 oz	goat cheese, crumbled	50 g

1. Boil or steam sweet potatoes about 8 minutes, or until tip of sharp knife pierces easily. Drain; mash with maple syrup and cinnamon.

2. In a nonstick frying pan sprayed with vegetable spray, heat oil over medium-high heat. Add garlic and onions; cook, stirring constantly, 1 minute. Stir into sweet potato mixture. Stir in coriander.

3. Lay 3 tortillas on a work surface. Divide sweet potato mixture evenly among tortillas and spread to edges. Sprinkle evenly with goat cheese. Lay remaining tortillas on top and press gently to stick.

4. Put on baking sheet. Bake 5 minutes or until hot. Use a sharp knife to slice into individual pieces.

PER SERVING (8)

Calories	198
Protein	4 g
Fat, total	4 g
Fat, saturated	1.0 g
Carbohydrates	37 g
Sodium	180 mg
Cholesterol	0 mg
Fiber	3 g

Tofu and Chickpea Garlic Dip

SERVES 6 TO 8

TIP

Tofu combined with beans, such as the chickpeas used here, gives the dip a butter-like texture.

Be sure to buy soft (silken) tofu to ensure a creamy dip. Firm or pressed tofu will result in a granular texture.

Tahini is a sesame paste found in the international section of grocery stores. If you can't find it, try using smooth peanut butter instead.

MAKE AHEAD

Prepare up to 1 day in advance. Mix before serving.

1 cup	canned chickpeas, rinsed and drained	250 mL
8 oz	soft (silken) tofu, drained	250 g
2 tbsp	tahini	25 mL
2 tbsp	freshly squeezed lemon juice	25 mL
1 tsp	minced garlic	5 mL
1/4 cup	chopped fresh dill (or 1 tsp [5 mL] dried)	50 mL
1/4 cup	chopped green onions	50 mL
1/4 cup	chopped green olives	50 mL
1/4 cup	chopped red bell peppers	50 mL
1/4 tsp	freshly ground black pepper	1 mL

1. In a food processor, combine chickpeas, tofu, tahini, lemon juice and garlic; purée. Stir in dill, green onions, olives, red peppers and pepper.

2. Chill. Serve with vegetables, crackers or bread.

PER SERVING (8)

Calories	86
Protein	5 g
Fat, total	4 g
Fat, saturated	1.0 g
Carbohydrates	8 g
Sodium	153 mg
Cholesterol	0 mg
Fiber	2 g

Sautéed Vegetable Feta Cheese Spread

◆■◆■◆■◆◀━━━▶■◆■◆■◆■◆

SERVES 6 TO 8

TIP

Pulse food processor on and off for a chunky texture.

Try goat cheese instead of feta.

For an attractive-looking spread, line a decorative mold with plastic wrap and unmold after chilled.

MAKE AHEAD

Prepare up to 2 days in advance.

1/2 cup	chopped carrots	125 mL
2 tsp	vegetable oil	10 mL
2 tsp	minced garlic	10 mL
3/4 cup	chopped red bell peppers	175 mL
3/4 cup	chopped leeks	175 mL
1/2 cup	chopped onions	125 mL
1/4 cup	sliced black olives	50 mL
2 tbsp	light sour cream	25 mL
2 tbsp	light mayonnaise	25 mL
1 tbsp	freshly squeezed lemon juice	15 mL
1/2 tsp	dried oregano	2 mL
2 oz	feta cheese, crumbled	50 g

1. Boil or steam carrots just until tender, about 5 minutes. Drain, and set aside.

2. In a saucepan heat oil over medium-low heat. Add garlic, red peppers, leeks, onions and carrots; cook, stirring occasionally, for 5 minutes or until tender. Cool.

3. In a food processor combine cooled vegetables, black olives, sour cream, mayonnaise, lemon juice, oregano and feta. Process to desired consistency. Serve with crackers or vegetables.

PER SERVING (8)	
Calories	72
Protein	2 g
Fat, total	4 g
Fat, saturated	1.0 g
Carbohydrates	8 g
Sodium	134 mg
Cholesterol	6 mg
Fiber	1 g

White Bean and Roasted Pepper Bruschetta

◆■◆■◆■◄━━━►■◆■◆■◆■

TIP

Tired of garlic bread? This is a great alternative.

If fresh basil is not available, substitute parsley.

Roast your own red bell peppers or buy water-packed roasted red peppers.

Double recipe and use as a dip.

MAKE AHEAD

Prepare bean mixture up to 1 day in advance.

Preheat oven 425° F (220° C)
Baking sheet

1 cup	canned white kidney beans, rinsed and drained,	1
1/4 cup	chopped fresh basil (or 1/2 tsp [2 mL] dried)	50 mL
1 1/2 tsp	freshly squeezed lemon juice	7 mL
1/2 tsp	minced garlic	2 mL
1/2 tsp	sesame oil	2 mL
1	baguette or thin French loaf	1
2 tbsp	chopped roasted red peppers	25 mL

1. In a food processor, purée beans, basil, lemon juice, garlic and sesame oil until smooth.

2. Slice baguette into 1-inch (2.5 cm) slices. In a toaster oven or under a preheated broiler, toast until golden; turn and toast opposite side. Spread each slice with approximately 1 1/2 tsp (7 mL) bean mixture. Top with chopped red peppers.

3. Bake until warm, approximately 5 minutes.

PER SERVING (8)

Calories	197
Protein	7 g
Fat, total	2 g
Fat, saturated	0.4 g
Carbohydrates	37 g
Sodium	385 mg
Cholesterol	0 mg
Fiber	3 g

CLOCKWISE FROM UPPER LEFT: MARINATED GREEK MUSHROOMS (PAGE 23) ➤
SAUTÉED VEGETABLE FETA CHEESE SPREAD (PAGE 31)
CAESAR TORTILLA PIZZAS (PAGE 17)

Leek Mushroom Cheese Pâté

TIP

If using wild mushrooms, try shiitake or cremini.

This can be served in a serving bowl instead of a loaf pan.

MAKE AHEAD

Prepare up to 2 days in advance.

9- by 5-inch (2 L) loaf pan lined with plastic wrap

2 tsp	vegetable oil	10 mL
1 1/2 tsp	minced garlic	7 mL
1 1/2 cups	chopped leeks	375 mL
1/2 cup	finely chopped carrots	125 mL
12 oz	oyster or regular mushrooms, thinly sliced	375 g
2 tbsp	sherry *or* white wine	25 mL
2 tbsp	chopped fresh dill (or 2 tsp [10 mL] dried)	25 mL
1 1/2 tsp	dried oregano	7 mL
1/4 tsp	coarsely ground black pepper	1 mL
2 oz	feta cheese, crumbled	50 g
2 oz	light cream cheese	50 g
1/2 cup	5% ricotta cheese	125 mL
2 tsp	freshly squeezed lemon juice	10 mL
2 tbsp	chopped fresh dill	25 mL

1. In a large nonstick frying pan sprayed with vegetable spray, heat oil over medium-high heat. Add garlic, leeks and carrots; cook 3 minutes, stirring occasionally. Stir in mushrooms, sherry, dill, oregano and pepper; cook, stirring occasionally, 8 to 10 minutes or until carrots are tender and liquid is absorbed. Remove from heat.

2. Transfer vegetable mixture to a food processor. Add feta, cream cheese, ricotta and lemon juice; purée until smooth. Spoon into prepared loaf pan. Cover and chill until firm.

3. Invert onto serving platter; sprinkle with chopped dill. Serve with crackers, bread or vegetables.

PER SERVING (10)	
Calories	75
Protein	4 g
Fat, total	3 g
Fat, saturated	2.0 g
Carbohydrates	6 g
Sodium	117 mg
Cholesterol	11 mg
Fiber	1 g

◄ TORTELLINI MINESTRONE WITH SPINACH (PAGE 52)

Rose's Famous Pizza

Preheat oven to 425° F (220° C)

Pizza pan

1	12-inch (30 cm) prebaked pizza crust	1
1/4 cup	pesto (see recipe, page 68)	50 mL
1 cup	sliced mushrooms	250 mL
1/2 cup	diced red bell peppers	125 mL
1/3 cup	chopped green onions	75 mL
1/4 cup	sliced black olives	50 mL
1 cup	shredded low-fat mozzarella cheese (about 4 oz [125 g])	250 mL
2 oz	feta cheese, crumbled	50 g

1. Place pizza crust on pizza pan. Spread with pesto. Sprinkle with mushrooms, red peppers, green onions, and olives. Top with mozzarella and feta cheeses.

2. Bake 20 minutes or until cheese is melted and bottom of crust is browned.

SOUPS

Artichoke Leek Potato Soup

TIP

This is an unusual, textured, great-tasting soup. A good source of fiber, too.

Replace tarragon with basil, dill, or parsley.

MAKE AHEAD

Prepare up to 2 days in advance.

Freeze up to 4 weeks.

PER SERVING

Calories	127
Protein	4 g
Fat, total	3 g
Fat, saturated	0.2 g
Carbohydrates	24 g
Sodium	236 mg
Cholesterol	0 mg
Fiber	5 g

STOCK TIPS

Use vegetable bouillon cubes, powder or canned vegetable bouillon.

Freeze in 1-cup (250 mL) portions; label and date.

Substitute other vegetables of your choice. Try fennel, mushrooms, leeks, potatoes, yams or lettuce.

2 tsp	vegetable oil	10 mL
2 tsp	minced garlic	10 mL
1 1/2 cups	chopped leeks	375 mL
3 1/2 to 4 cups	BASIC VEGETABLE STOCK (see recipe, below)	875 mL to 1 L
1 1/2 cups	diced potatoes	375 mL
1 tsp	dried tarragon	5 mL
1	can (14 oz [398 mL]) artichoke hearts, drained and halved	1

1. In a nonstick saucepan, heat oil over medium-low heat. Stir in garlic and leeks, cover and cook 5 minutes.

2. Stir in stock, potatoes, tarragon and artichoke hearts. Bring to a boil; reduce heat to medium-low, cover and cook 15 minutes, or until potato is tender.

3. In a food processor or blender, purée soup.

Basic Vegetable Stock

8 cups	fresh water *or* cooking water	2 L
2	stalks celery, chopped	2
2	large onions, chopped	2
2	large carrots, washed and chopped	2
4	cloves garlic, chopped	4
4	bay leaves	4
4	whole cloves (or pinch ground)	4
10	peppercorns, crushed	10
1/4 cup	chopped fresh parsley (or 1/4 tsp [1 mL] dried)	50 mL
1/4 tsp	salt (optional)	1 mL

1. Combine all ingredients in a large pot. Bring to a simmer and cook, uncovered, for 45 minutes.

2. Remove from heat; let cool. Strain, discarding solids. Store in a container with tight-fitting lid. Stock will keep 1 week in refrigerator and several months if frozen.

Corn, Tomato and Zucchini Soup

TIP

Try grilling or barbecuing corn on the cob until charred. Remove kernels with a knife.

Fresh basil as a garnish is excellent.

Great soup in just under 30 minutes.

MAKE AHEAD

Prepare up to 2 days in advance. Add more stock if necessary when reheating.

Freeze for up to 3 weeks.

2 tsp	vegetable oil	10 mL
1 tsp	minced garlic	5 mL
3 cups	diced zucchini	750 mL
1 1/2 cups	chopped onions	375 mL
3 cups	BASIC VEGETABLE STOCK (see recipe, page 36)	750 mL
1	can (19 oz [540 mL]) whole tomatoes	1
1 1/4 cups	frozen or canned corn, drained	300 mL
2 tsp	dried basil	10 mL

1. In a nonstick saucepan sprayed with vegetable spray, heat oil over medium-high heat. Add garlic, zucchini and onions; cook for 5 minutes or until softened.

2. Stir in stock, tomatoes, corn, and basil. Bring to a boil, reduce heat to low and simmer 20 minutes, breaking up whole tomatoes with the back of a spoon.

PER SERVING (6)

Calories	106
Protein	4 g
Fat, total	2 g
Fat, saturated	0.2 g
Carbohydrates	22 g
Sodium	159 mg
Cholesterol	0 mg
Fiber	4 g

Cold Two-Melon Soup

6 cups	cubed ripe honeydew or other green melon	1.5 L
2 tsp	grated lime zest	10 mL
1/4 cup	freshly squeezed lime juice	50 mL
1/4 cup	granulated sugar	50 mL
3 cups	cubed ripe cantaloupe	750 mL
1 tbsp	orange juice concentrate	15 mL
1 tsp	grated orange zest	5 mL
	Mint sprigs	

1. In a food processor purée honeydew melon, lime zest, lime juice, and 2 tbsp (25 mL) of the sugar until smooth. Transfer to a bowl.

2. Rinse out bowl of food processor. Add cantaloupe, orange juice concentrate, orange zest and remaining sugar; purée until smooth. Transfer to a separate bowl.

3. Chill both soups 30 minutes or until cold.

4. To serve, ladle 1 cup (250 mL) green soup into each of 4 individual serving bowls. Carefully pour 1/2 cup (125 mL) orange soup into the center. Garnish with mint sprigs and serve.

Cold Mango Soup

TIP

Try to ensure that mango is ripe. If not, add some sugar to taste.

This soup can also be served at room temperature.

MAKE AHEAD

Prepare up to 2 days in advance.

Freeze up to 3 weeks.

2 tsp	vegetable oil	10 mL
1/2 cup	chopped onions	125 mL
2 tsp	minced garlic	10 mL
2 cups	BASIC VEGETABLE STOCK (see recipe, page 36)	500 mL
2 1/2 cups	chopped ripe mango (about 2 large)	625 mL

Garnish (optional)

2% plain yogurt

Coriander leaves

1. In a nonstick saucepan, heat oil over medium heat. Add onions and garlic; cook, stirring, 4 minutes or until browned.

2. Add stock. Bring to a boil; reduce heat to medium-low and cook 5 minutes or until onions are soft.

3. Transfer mixture to a food processor. Add 2 cups (500 mL) of the mango. Purée until smooth. Stir in remaining chopped mango.

4. Chill 2 hours or until cold. Serve with a dollop of yogurt and garnish with coriander, if desired.

PER SERVING	
Calories	99
Protein	1 g
Fat, total	3 g
Fat, saturated	0.2 g
Carbohydrates	20 g
Sodium	7 mg
Cholesterol	0 mg
Fiber	3 g

Leek, Fennel and Butternut Squash Minestrone

TIP

Fennel is now available in most groceries or fruit markets. If unavailable, use celery and increase fennel seed to 1 1/2 tsp (7 mL).

This soup is a great variation on regular minestrone.

MAKE AHEAD

Prepare early in the day. Add pasta to cook just before serving. Add more stock if reheating.

2 tsp	vegetable oil	10 mL
2 tsp	minced garlic	10 mL
2 cups	sliced mushrooms	500 mL
2 cups	thinly sliced green cabbage	500 mL
1 1/2 cups	chopped leeks	375 mL
6 1/2 cups	BASIC VEGETABLE STOCK (see recipe, page 36)	1.625 L
2 cups	cubed butternut squash	500 mL
1 cup	chopped fennel bulb	250 mL
1 tsp	fennel seeds	5 mL
1 cup	diced plum tomatoes	250 mL
2 oz	linguine, broken	50 g

Garnish (optional)

3 tbsp	grated Parmesan cheese	45 mL

1. In a nonstick saucepan sprayed with vegetable spray, heat oil over medium-high heat. Add garlic, mushrooms, cabbage and leeks; cook 5 minutes or until cabbage is wilted and vegetables are softened.

2. Stir in stock, squash, fennel bulb and fennel seed. Bring to a boil; reduce heat to medium-low, cover and cook 10 minutes until squash is tender. Stir in tomatoes and linguine; cover and cook 8 to 10 minutes or until vegetables are tender and pasta is tender but firm.

3. Serve immediately, garnished with Parmesan, if desired.

PER SERVING (8)	
Calories	82
Protein	3 g
Fat, total	2 g
Fat, saturated	0.1 g
Carbohydrates	16 g
Sodium	24 mg
Cholesterol	0 mg
Fiber	2 g

Wild Mushroom and Barley Soup

TIP

Oyster or cremini mushrooms are the best to use here. If unavailable, substitute white common mushrooms.

Barley is available in "pearl" and "pot" varieties; whichever you use, cook until tender.

This soup is a good source of fiber.

Use some dried mushrooms to really highlight this dish.

MAKE AHEAD

Prepare up to 2 days in advance. Add more stock when reheating if too thick.

Freeze for up to 3 weeks.

2 tsp	vegetable oil	10 mL
2 tsp	minced garlic	10 mL
1 cup	chopped onions	250 mL
3 1/2 cups	BASIC VEGETABLE STOCK (see recipe, page 36)	875 mL
1	can (19 oz [540 mL]) tomatoes, crushed	1
1/2 cup	barley	125 mL
1/2 tsp	dried thyme	2 mL
1/4 tsp	freshly ground black pepper	1 mL
8 oz	wild mushrooms, sliced (see Tip, at left)	250 g

1. In a nonstick saucepan, heat oil over medium heat. Add garlic and onions; cook 4 minutes or until softened.

2. Stir in stock, tomatoes, barley, thyme and pepper. Bring to a boil; reduce heat to medium-low, cover and simmer 40 to 50 minutes, or until barley is tender.

3. Meanwhile, in a nonstick frying pan sprayed with vegetable spray, cook mushrooms over high heat, stirring, 8 minutes or until browned.

4. Stir mushrooms into soup and serve.

PER SERVING (6)	
Calories	173
Protein	6 g
Fat, total	3 g
Fat, saturated	0.3 g
Carbohydrates	33 g
Sodium	236 mg
Cholesterol	0 mg
Fiber	7 g

Pumpkin and White Bean Soup

TIP

In season, use fresh pumpkin. Bake approximately 1 hour at 375° F (190°C) or until tender.

If white kidney beans are unavailable, try small navy beans or chickpeas.

Maple syrup adds a subtle sweetness, unlike sugar.

This soup is a good source of fiber.

MAKE AHEAD

Prepare up to 2 days in advance. Add more stock if too thick.

Freeze for up to 4 weeks.

2 tsp	vegetable oil	10 mL
2 tsp	minced garlic	10 mL
1 cup	chopped onions	250 mL
1/2 cup	chopped carrots	125 mL
1/2 cup	chopped celery	125 mL
3 1/2 cups	BASIC VEGETABLE STOCK (see recipe, page 36)	875 mL
1	can (14 oz [398 mL]) pumpkin (not pie filling)	1
1	can (19 oz [540 mL]) white kidney beans, rinsed and drained	1
1	bay leaf	1
1 tsp	ground ginger	5 mL
1/4 cup	maple syrup	50 mL

1. In a nonstick saucepan sprayed with vegetable spray, heat oil over medium-high heat. Add garlic, onions, carrots and celery; cook 4 minutes or until onions and celery are softened.

2. Stir in stock, pumpkin, beans, bay leaf and ginger. Bring to a boil; reduce heat, cover, and cook 15 to 20 minutes or until vegetables are tender.

3. Stir in maple syrup. Serve immediately.

PER SERVING (6)

Calories	175
Protein	7 g
Fat, total	2 g
Fat, saturated	0.3 g
Carbohydrates	34 g
Sodium	172 mg
Cholesterol	0 mg
Fiber	6 g

Red Onion and Grilled Red Pepper Soup

TIP

Sweet bell peppers and red onions make this a naturally sweet-tasting soup. Sugar may not be necessary.

Start with the lesser amount of stock, adding more to reach the consistency you prefer.

This soup is a good source of fiber.

MAKE AHEAD

Prepare up to 2 days in advance. Add more stock if too thick.

Freeze up to 4 weeks.

Preheat oven to broil
Baking sheet

3	large red bell peppers	3
2 tsp	vegetable oil	10 mL
2 tsp	minced garlic	10 mL
1 tbsp	packed brown sugar	15 mL
5 cups	thinly sliced red onions	1.25 L
3 to 3 1/2 cups	BASIC VEGETABLE STOCK (see recipe, page 36)	750 mL to 875 mL

Garnish

1/3 cup	chopped fresh basil *or* parsley	75 mL
	Light sour cream (optional)	

1. Arrange oven rack 6 inches (15 cm) under element. Cook peppers on baking sheet, turning occasionally, 20 minutes or until charred. Cool. Discard stem, skin and seeds; cut peppers into thin strips. Set aside.

2. In a large nonstick saucepan, heat oil over medium-low heat. Add garlic, brown sugar and red onions; cook, stirring occasionally, 15 minutes or until onions are browned. Stir in stock and red pepper strips; cook 15 minutes longer.

3. In a blender or food processor, purée soup until smooth. Serve hot, garnished with chopped basil or parsley and a dollop of sour cream, if desired.

PER SERVING

Calories	129
Protein	3 g
Fat, total	3 g
Fat, saturated	0.2 g
Carbohydrates	25 g
Sodium	15 mg
Cholesterol	0 mg
Fiber	5 g

Roasted Eggplant and Bell Pepper Soup

Serves 4 to 6

TIP

This combination of eggplant and sweet peppers is unusual and delicious.

Start with the smaller amount of stock, adding more if soup is too thick.

MAKE AHEAD

Prepare up to 2 days in advance, adding more stock if necessary.

Freeze up to 4 weeks.

PER SERVING (6)	
Calories	82
Protein	3 g
Fat, total	2 g
Fat, saturated	0.3 g
Carbohydrates	15 g
Sodium	26 mg
Cholesterol	1 mg
Fiber	4 g

Preheat broiler

Baking sheet

1	medium eggplant (about 1 lb [500 g]), cut in half lengthwise	1
1	medium red or yellow bell pepper	1
2 tsp	vegetable oil	10 mL
2 tsp	minced garlic	10 mL
1 1/2 cups	chopped leeks	375 mL
1/2 cup	chopped onions	125 mL
2 1/2 to 3 cups	BASIC VEGETABLE STOCK (see recipe, page 36)	625 to 750 mL
1 cup	diced tomatoes	250 mL
2 tbsp	tomato paste	25 mL
2	bay leaves	2
1/3 cup	2% milk *or* BASIC VEGETABLE STOCK	75 mL

Garnish

1/3 cup	chopped fresh basil *or* parsley	75 mL
1/4 cup	light sour cream (optional)	50 mL

1. Put eggplant and pepper on baking sheet. With rack 6 inches (15 cm) under broiler, cook about 20 minutes, turning occasionally, until pepper is charred. Remove pepper; continue cooking eggplant 10 minutes longer or until very soft. Cool. Peel, stem, seed and chop pepper; scoop pulp out of eggplant shell, including seeds. Set aside chopped pepper and eggplant pulp.

2. In a nonstick saucepan, heat oil over medium heat. Add garlic, leeks and onions; cook 5 minutes or until softened. Stir in stock, tomatoes, tomato paste and bay leaves. Bring to a boil; reduce heat to medium-low, cover and cook 10 minutes.

3. In food processor or blender, purée soup with roasted eggplant and pepper. Add milk or stock.

4. Serve hot, garnished with chopped basil and a dollop of sour cream, if desired.

Roasted Tomato and Corn Soup

◆▢◆▢◆▢◆▢◆◀━━▶◆▢◆▢◆▢◆▢◆

SERVES 4 TO 6

TIP

Regular fresh tomatoes can replace plum.

Dill or coriander can replace basil.

In the summer, grill tomatoes and 2 whole cobs of corn on barbecue.

MAKE AHEAD

Prepare soup up to 2 days in advance, adding more stock, if necessary, when reheating.

Freeze up to 4 weeks.

PER SERVING (6)

Calories	117
Protein	4 g
Fat, total	3 g
Fat, saturated	0.3 g
Carbohydrates	23 g
Sodium	173 mg
Cholesterol	0 mg
Fiber	4 g

Preheat broiler

Two baking sheets lined with aluminum foil and sprayed with vegetable spray

2 1/2 lbs	plum tomatoes (about 10)	1.25 kg
1	can (12 oz [341 mL]) corn, drained	1
2 tsp	vegetable oil	10 mL
2 tsp	minced garlic	10 mL
1 cup	chopped onions	250 mL
3/4 cup	finely chopped carrots	175 mL
2 1/2 cups	BASIC VEGETABLE STOCK (see recipe, page 36)	625 mL
3 tbsp	tomato paste	45 mL
1/2 cup	chopped fresh basil (or 2 tsp [10 mL] dried)	125 mL

1. Put tomatoes on one baking sheet. With rack 6 inches (15 cm) under broiler, broil tomatoes about 30 minutes, turning occasionally, or until charred on all sides. Meanwhile, spread corn on other baking sheet and broil, stirring occasionally, about 15 minutes or until slightly browned. (Some corn kernels will pop.) When cool enough to handle, chop tomatoes.

2. In a nonstick saucepan, heat oil over medium-high heat. Add garlic, onions and carrots; cook 5 minutes or until softened and beginning to brown. Add roasted tomatoes, stock, tomato paste and, if using, dried basil. (If using fresh basil, wait until Step 3.) Bring to a boil; reduce heat to medium-low, cover and cook 20 minutes or until vegetables tender.

3. In food processor or blender, purée soup. Return to saucepan; stir in corn and, if using, fresh basil.

Roasted Vegetable Soup

SERVES 6 TO 8

TIP

Here's an easy, delicious soup using roasting as a great alternative to other methods of cooking. Roasting gives a smoky flavor to foods.

Other vegetables can be substituted. Keep amounts the same.

Start with smaller amount of stock, adding more if soup is too thick.

MAKE AHEAD

Prepare soup up to 2 days in advance. Add more stock if necessary.

Freeze up to 4 weeks.

Preheat oven to 425° F (220° C)
Roasting pan sprayed with vegetable spray

2	heads garlic	2
2	medium carrots, peeled	2
1	medium zucchini	1
2	medium leeks, white parts only	2
1	large red bell pepper	1
12 oz	plum tomatoes	375 g
1	medium sweet potato, peeled	1
1	medium red onion, peeled	1
1 tbsp	olive oil	15 mL
5 1/2 cups	BASIC VEGETABLE STOCK (approx.) (see recipe, page 36)	1.375 L
1 tsp	dried basil	5 mL
1/2 tsp	coarsely ground black pepper	2 mL

1. Slice top off each head of garlic. Cut carrots and zucchini in half lengthwise; cut into large pieces. Cut leeks in half lengthwise; wash carefully then cut into large pieces. Stem, seed and quarter red pepper. Cut tomatoes, sweet potato and onion into wedges. Put all vegetables in roasting pan; toss with olive oil.

2. Bake 1 hour, tossing occasionally, or until vegetables are tender.

3. Squeeze garlic out of skins. Put in a food processor with rest of roasted vegetables. Purée until finely chopped. Add stock, basil and black pepper; purée in 2 batches until smooth. Add extra stock until desired consistency is reached. Transfer to a large saucepan; heat gently until hot. Serve.

PER SERVING (8)

Calories	98
Protein	2 g
Fat, total	2 g
Fat, saturated	0.3 g
Carbohydrates	19 g
Sodium	27 mg
Cholesterol	0 mg
Fiber	3 g

Split-Pea Barley Vegetable Soup

◆■◆■◆■ ◄■■■■► ■◆■◆■◆■◆

TIP

Substitute green split peas if desired. The yellow variety is widely available.

Barley is available in "pearl" and "pot" varieties; whichever you use, cook until tender.

Broccoli or yellow beans can substitute for green beans.

MAKE AHEAD

Prepare Steps 1 and 2 up to 1 day in advance. Add beans and tomatoes when reheating and ready to serve.

Can freeze up to 3 weeks.

1 tsp	vegetable oil	5 mL
1 1/2 tsp	minced garlic	7 mL
3/4 cup	chopped onions	175 mL
6 cups	BASIC VEGETABLE STOCK (see recipe, page 36)	1.5 L
1 1/2 cups	diced potatoes	375 mL
1 cup	diced carrots	250 mL
1/2 cup	dried yellow split peas	125 mL
1/3 cup	barley	75 mL
2	bay leaves	2
2 tsp	dried basil	10 mL
1 1/2 cups	green beans cut in 1-inch (2.5 cm) pieces	375 mL
1 cup	diced plum tomatoes	250 mL
1/4 tsp	freshly ground black pepper	1 mL

1. In a nonstick saucepan sprayed with vegetable spray, heat oil over medium heat. Add garlic and onions; cook 4 minutes or until softened.

2. Stir in stock, potatoes, carrots, split peas, barley, bay leaves and basil. Bring to a boil; reduce heat to medium-low, cover and cook 40 minutes or until peas and barley are tender.

3. Stir in green beans, tomatoes and pepper; cook, covered, 10 minutes or until green beans are tender-crisp.

PER SERVING (8)	
Calories	129
Protein	6 g
Fat, total	1 g
Fat, saturated	0.1 g
Carbohydrates	26 g
Sodium	20 mg
Cholesterol	0 mg
Fiber	4 g

Squash and Carrot Soup

2 tsp	vegetable oil	10 mL
1 1/2 tsp	minced garlic	7 mL
1 1/2 cups	sliced leeks	375 mL
6 cups	chopped butternut squash (about 1 3/4 lb [875 g])	1.5 L
3 1/2 to 4 1/2 cups	BASIC VEGETABLE STOCK (see recipe, page 36)	875 mL to 1.125 L
1 cup	diced carrots	250 mL
1/2 tsp	dried thyme	2 mL

Garnish (optional)

2% plain yogurt
or light sour cream

1. In a nonstick saucepan sprayed with vegetable spray, heat oil over medium-low heat. Stir in garlic and leeks; cook, covered, for 5 minutes or until softened.

2. Stir in squash, stock, carrots and thyme. Bring to a boil; reduce heat to medium-low, cover and cook 12 to 15 minutes or until vegetables are tender.

3. Transfer soup to a food processor or blender. Purée until smooth. Serve with a dollop of yogurt or sour cream, if desired.

PER SERVING (6)	
Calories	106
Protein	2 g
Fat, total	2 g
Fat, saturated	0.2 g
Carbohydrates	23 g
Sodium	23 mg
Cholesterol	0 mg
Fiber	1 g

Sweet Potato Orange Soup with Maple Syrup

TIP

Freshly squeezed juice is the best to use. Use orange from which you obtained the zest.

Maple syrup adds a subtle sweetness, unlike sugar.

This soup is a good source of fiber.

MAKE AHEAD

Prepare up to 2 days in advance, adding more stock when reheating.

Freeze up to 3 weeks.

1 tsp	vegetable oil	5 mL
1 1/2 tsp	minced garlic	7 mL
3/4 cup	chopped onions	175 mL
1 3/4 lbs	sweet potatoes, peeled and chopped (about 6 cups [1.5 L])	875 g
3 1/2 cups	BASIC VEGETABLE STOCK (see recipe, page 36)	875 mL
2	bay leaves	2
1 tbsp	grated orange zest	15 mL
1/2 cup	orange juice	125 mL
3 tbsp	maple syrup	45 mL

1. In a nonstick saucepan sprayed with vegetable spray, heat oil over medium heat. Add garlic and onions; cook 4 minutes or until softened.

2. Stir in sweet potatoes, stock and bay leaves. Bring to a boil; reduce heat to medium-low, cover and cook 20 minutes or until sweet potatoes are tender. Remove bay leaves.

3. In a food processor or blender, purée soup along with orange zest, orange juice and maple syrup until smooth.

PER SERVING (6)

Calories	203
Protein	3 g
Fat, total	1 g
Fat, saturated	0.2 g
Carbohydrates	46 g
Sodium	25 mg
Cholesterol	0 mg
Fiber	5 g

Eggplant Tortellini Tomato Soup

SERVES 6 TO 8

TIP

Substitute onions for leeks.

Ravioli or gnocchi can replace tortellini.

MAKE AHEAD

Prepare up to 2 days in advance, but do not add tortellini until ready to re-heat and serve.

Can be frozen up to 4 weeks.

2 tsp	vegetable oil	10 mL
2 tsp	minced garlic	10 mL
4 cups	peeled chopped eggplant	1 L
2 1/2 cups	chopped leeks	625 mL
1	can (19 oz [540 mL]) tomatoes, puréed	1
3 cups	BASIC VEGETABLE STOCK (see recipe, page 36)	750 mL
2 tbsp	tomato paste	25 mL
1 1/2 tsp	dried basil	7 mL
1	bay leaf	1
4 oz	frozen cheese tortellini	125 g
	Grated Parmesan cheese (optional)	

1. In a nonstick saucepan sprayed with vegetable spray, heat oil over medium-high heat. Add garlic, eggplant and leeks; cook, stirring frequently, 8 minutes or until vegetables are softened.

2. Stir in tomatoes, stock, tomato paste, basil and bay leaf; bring to a boil, reduce heat to medium-low, cover and cook 15 minutes, or until eggplant is very tender.

3. In a food processor or blender, purée soup. Return to saucepan; bring to a boil. Stir in tortellini; reduce heat to medium and cook 8 minutes or until tortellini is tender.

4. Serve hot, sprinkled with Parmesan, if desired.

PER SERVING (8)

Calories	103
Protein	4 g
Fat, total	2 g
Fat, saturated	0.3 g
Carbohydrates	18 g
Sodium	187 mg
Cholesterol	0 mg
Fiber	3 g

Yellow Split-Pea Soup

SERVES 6 TO 8

TIP

The yellow split peas puréed in this soup give it a rich and creamy texture.

Add fresh herbs such as dill, basil or parsley as a garnish.

MAKE AHEAD

Prepare up to 2 days in advance, adding more stock if too thick.

Freeze up to 4 weeks.

2 tsp	vegetable oil	10 mL
2 tsp	minced garlic	10 mL
1 cup	chopped onions	250 mL
1 cup	chopped carrots	250 mL
1 cup	chopped celery	250 mL
7 cups	BASIC VEGETABLE STOCK (see recipe, page 36)	1.75 L
1 cup	diced potatoes	250 mL
1 cup	dried yellow split peas	250 mL

Garnish

| 1/4 cup | 2% plain yogurt (optional) | 50 mL |
| 1/4 cup | chopped green onions | 50 mL |

1. In a nonstick saucepan, heat oil over medium-high heat. Add garlic, onions, carrots and celery; cook 5 minutes or until vegetables are softened and starting to brown.

2. Stir in stock, potatoes and split peas. Bring to a boil; reduce heat to medium-low, cover and cook 40 minutes or until split peas are tender.

3. In a food processor or blender, purée soup. Serve hot with a dollop of yogurt, if desired, and sprinkled with green onions.

PER SERVING (8)	
Calories	136
Protein	8 g
Fat, total	2 g
Fat, saturated	0.2 g
Carbohydrates	24 g
Sodium	32 mg
Cholesterol	0 mg
Fiber	2 g

Tortellini Minestrone with Spinach

TIP

Try ravioli or gnocchi instead of tortellini.

If fresh spinach is unavailable, substitute one-quarter 10-oz (300 g) package frozen spinach. Thaw and drain excess liquid.

Plum tomatoes can be replaced with the regular variety.

MAKE AHEAD

Prepare soup up to 2 days in advance, but do not add tortellini until ready to re-heat and serve.

Can be frozen up to 3 weeks.

2 tsp	vegetable oil	10 mL
2 tsp	minced garlic	10 mL
1 cup	chopped onions	250 mL
1/2 cup	chopped carrots	125 mL
1/2 cup	chopped celery	125 mL
4 cups	BASIC VEGETABLE STOCK (see recipe, page 36)	1 L
1 tsp	dried basil	5 mL
1/4 tsp	freshly ground black pepper	1 mL
1 1/2 cups	diced plum tomatoes	375 mL
2 cups	chopped fresh spinach	500 mL
2 cups	frozen cheese tortellini	500 mL
3 tbsp	grated Parmesan cheese	45 mL

1. In a nonstick saucepan sprayed with vegetable spray, heat oil over medium-high heat. Add garlic, onions, carrots and celery; cook 4 minutes or until onions are softened.

2. Add stock, basil and pepper. Bring to a boil; reduce heat to medium and cook 8 minutes or until vegetables are tender-crisp.

3. Stir in tomatoes, spinach and tortellini. Cover and cook 5 minutes or until tortellini is heated through and vegetables are tender. Serve immediately, garnished with Parmesan cheese.

PER SERVING (6)	
Calories	157
Protein	7 g
Fat, total	5 g
Fat, saturated	1.0 g
Carbohydrates	23 g
Sodium	234 mg
Cholesterol	3 mg
Fiber	3 g

SAUCES

Balsamic Orange Vinaigrette

**MAKES 2/3 CUP
(150 mL)**

TIP

Great over leafy lettuce or spinach.

For a stronger orange flavor, add 1 tsp (5 mL) grated orange zest.

MAKE AHEAD

Prepare up to 2 days in advance.

1/4 cup	chopped fresh parsley	50 mL
3 tbsp	vegetable oil	45 mL
3 tbsp	balsamic vinegar	45 mL
3 tbsp	minced red onions	45 mL
2 tbsp	orange juice concentrate	25 mL
1 tbsp	packed brown sugar	15 mL
1 tsp	minced garlic	5 mL

1. In a small bowl, whisk together parsley, oil, vinegar, red onions, orange juice concentrate, sugar and garlic.

PER TBSP (15 mL)	
Calories	53
Protein	0 g
Fat, total	5 g
Fat, saturated	0.3 g
Carbohydrates	3 g
Sodium	1 mg
Cholesterol	0 mg
Fiber	0 g

Black and White Bean Salsa

1 cup	canned black beans, rinsed and drained	250 mL
1 cup	canned navy beans, rinsed and drained	250 mL
1 cup	chopped plum tomatoes	250 mL
1/2 cup	canned corn, drained	125 mL
1/3 cup	chopped fresh coriander	75 mL
1/3 cup	chopped green onions	75 mL
1/3 cup	chopped red bell peppers	75 mL
2 tbsp	freshly squeezed lime juice	25 mL
1 1/2 tbsp	olive oil	22 mL
1 1/2 tsp	chili powder	7 mL
1 tsp	minced garlic	5 mL
	Freshly ground black pepper to taste	

1. In a bowl combine black beans, navy beans, toma-
    to, corn, coriander, green onions, red peppers, lime
    juice, olive oil, chili powder and garlic; mix well.
    Season to taste with pepper.

PER 1/2 CUP (125 mL)	
Calories	147
Protein	7 g
Fat, total	4 g
Fat, saturated	1.0 g
Carbohydrates	23 g
Sodium	211 mg
Cholesterol	0 mg
Fiber	1 g

Chili Tomato Dressing

TIP

Try this gazpacho-type dressing over large chunks of vegetables.

For a spicier flavor, substitute vegetable cocktail for the tomato juice.

MAKE AHEAD

Prepare up to 2 days in advance.

1/2 cup	tomato juice	125 mL
3 tbsp	chili sauce	45 mL
2 tbsp	light mayonnaise	25 mL
1/4 cup	finely chopped cucumber	50 mL
3 tbsp	finely chopped onions	45 mL
3 tbsp	minced fresh parsley *or* basil	45 mL
2 tbsp	vegetable oil	25 mL
1 tbsp	balsamic vinegar	15 mL
3/4 tsp	minced garlic	4 mL

1. In a bowl whisk together tomato juice, chili sauce and mayonnaise. Stir in cucumber, onions, parsley, oil, vinegar and garlic.

PER TBSP (15 mL)	
Calories	14
Protein	0 g
Fat, total	1 g
Fat, saturated	0.1 g
Carbohydrates	1 g
Sodium	51 mg
Cholesterol	0 mg
Fiber	0 g

Creamy Italian Dressing

**MAKES 1/2 CUP
(125 mL)**

TIP

Delicious as a substitute for a Caesar dressing.

Use over salad greens and steamed vegetables.

MAKE AHEAD

Prepare up to 2 days in advance. Stir well before using.

2 tbsp	vegetable oil	25 mL
2 tbsp	light sour cream	25 mL
2 tbsp	water	25 mL
1 tbsp	light mayonnaise	15 mL
1 tbsp	balsamic vinegar *or* red wine vinegar	15 mL
1 tbsp	grated Parmesan cheese	15 mL
1 tsp	minced garlic	5 mL

1. In a small bowl, whisk together oil, sour cream, water, mayonnaise, vinegar, Parmesan and garlic.

PER TBSP (15 mL)	
Calories	38
Protein	1 g
Fat, total	4 g
Fat, saturated	0.4 g
Carbohydrates	1 g
Sodium	31 mg
Cholesterol	1 mg
Fiber	0 g

Creamy Parmesan Dressing

TIP

Capers gives this
dressing a real punch.
Omit them if you want a
milder flavor.

Ricotta cheese gives a
smoother consistency. If
using cottage cheese,
purée longer.

MAKE AHEAD

Prepare up to 2 days
in advance. Stir well
before using.

1/3 cup	5% ricotta *or* 2% cottage cheese (see Tip, at left)	75 mL
1/3 cup	light sour cream	75 mL
1/4 cup	grated Parmesan cheese	50 mL
1/4 cup	2% milk	50 mL
2 tbsp	freshly squeezed lemon juice	25 mL
1 tbsp	drained capers	15 mL
1 tsp	minced garlic	5 mL
1/8 tsp	freshly ground black pepper	0.5 mL

1. In a food processor combine ricotta cheese, sour cream, Parmesan, milk, lemon juice, capers, garlic and pepper; purée.

PER TBSP (15 mL)	
Calories	17
Protein	2 g
Fat, total	1 g
Fat, saturated	1 g
Carbohydrates	1 g
Sodium	35 mg
Cholesterol	3 mg
Fiber	0 g

Creamy Poppy Seed Dressing

MAKES 3/4 CUP (175 mL)

TIP

Serve as a dipping sauce for fruit spears or serve over a salad of spinach, orange slices and red onions.

This a great recipe for those who like sweet dressings rather than tart.

MAKE AHEAD

Prepare up to 2 days in advance.

1/4 cup	orange juice	50 mL
3 tbsp	light mayonnaise	45 mL
3 tbsp	light sour cream	45 mL
1 tbsp	honey	15 mL
2 tsp	poppy seeds	10 mL
1 tsp	grated orange zest	5 mL

1. In a small bowl, whisk together orange juice, mayonnaise, sour cream, honey, poppy seeds and orange zest.

PER TBSP (15 mL)	
Calories	26
Protein	0 g
Fat, total	1 g
Fat, saturated	0.1 g
Carbohydrates	3 g
Sodium	34 mg
Cholesterol	0 mg
Fiber	0 g

Creamy Russian Dressing

TIP

Use as a sandwich spread with bean burgers.

Great as a dip for vegetables or over green salad.

Similar to a Thousand Island dressing, but lighter.

MAKE AHEAD

Prepare up to 3 days in advance. Stir well before serving.

1/2 cup	light mayonnaise	125 mL
1/2 cup	light sour cream	125 mL
1/3 cup	chili sauce	75 mL
3 tbsp	minced green peppers	45 mL
3 tbsp	minced red bell peppers	45 mL
3 tbsp	minced red onions	45 mL

1. In a bowl stir together mayonnaise, sour cream, chili sauce, green and red peppers and red onions.

PER TBSP (15 mL)

Calories	24
Protein	0 g
Fat, total	1 g
Fat, saturated	0.1 g
Carbohydrates	3 g
Sodium	91 mg
Cholesterol	0.2 mg
Fiber	0 g

Creamy Tahini Lemon Dressing

MAKES 1 CUP (250 mL)

TIP

Serve with falafel.

Great over BEAN BURGERS (see recipe, page 99) or CHICKPEA TOFU BURGERS (see recipe, page 102).

Toss a combination of cooked beans together and use this as a dressing.

If tahini is unavailable, substitute creamy peanut butter.

MAKE AHEAD

Prepare up to 2 days in advance. Stir well before using.

1/3 cup	BASIC VEGETABLE STOCK (see recipe, page 36)	75 mL
1/3 cup	5% ricotta *or* 2% cottage cheese	75 mL
2 tbsp	tahini	25 mL
2 tbsp	light mayonnaise	25 mL
2 tbsp	olive oil	25 mL
1 tbsp	freshly squeezed lemon juice	15 mL
1 tbsp	soya sauce	15 mL
1 tsp	minced garlic	5 mL
1/4 cup	chopped fresh coriander	50 mL

1. In a food processor combine stock, ricotta, tahini, mayonnaise, olive oil, lemon juice, soya sauce and garlic; process until smooth. Stir in coriander.

PER TBSP (15 mL)

Calories	33
Protein	1 g
Fat, total	3 g
Fat, saturated	1 g
Carbohydrates	1 g
Sodium	84 mg
Cholesterol	1 mg
Fiber	0 g

Cucumber, Green Onion and Red Pepper Sauce

MAKES 1 CUP (250 mL), SERVING 3

TIP

Serve over cold cooked vegetables.

Great over BEAN BURGERS (see recipe, page 99) or CHICKPEA TOFU BURGERS (see recipe, page 102).

MAKE AHEAD

Prepare up to a day in advance; stir well before serving.

1/4 cup	chopped fresh dill	50 mL
1/4 cup	light sour cream	50 mL
3 tbsp	BASIC VEGETABLE STOCK (see recipe, page 36)	45 mL
3 tbsp	chopped green onions	45 mL
2 tbsp	light mayonnaise	25 mL
1 tbsp	freshly squeezed lemon juice	15 mL
1 tsp	minced garlic	5 mL
1/3 cup	chopped celery	75 mL
1/3 cup	chopped unpeeled cucumbers	75 mL
1/4 cup	chopped red bell peppers	50 mL

1. In a food processor, combine dill, sour cream, stock, green onions, mayonnaise, lemon juice and garlic; purée. Add celery, cucumbers and red peppers; pulse on and off until well mixed and chunky.

PER SERVING	
Calories	47
Protein	1 g
Fat, total	2 g
Fat, saturated	0.2 g
Carbohydrates	6 g
Sodium	80 mg
Cholesterol	1 mg
Fiber	1 g

Curry Vegetable Sauce

TIP

Serve over pasta, rice or another grain for a quick meal.

Excellent over hot steamed vegetables.

Try adding chopped dried fruits such as apricots, dates or raisins.

MAKE AHEAD

Prepare up to 2 days in advance and reheat adding more stock if too thick.

1 tbsp	margarine *or* butter	15 mL
1 cup	chopped onions	250 mL
1	carrot, finely chopped	1
1	stalk celery, chopped	1
1 tsp	minced garlic	5 mL
2 tbsp	all-purpose flour	25 mL
2 tsp	curry powder or to taste	10 mL
1 cup	BASIC VEGETABLE STOCK (see recipe, page 36)	250 mL
1 cup	2% milk	250 mL
	Freshly ground black pepper, to taste	

1. In a nonstick saucepan, melt margarine over medium-high heat. Add onions, carrot, celery and garlic; cook, stirring occasionally, 10 minutes or until soft and browned. Stir in flour and curry powder; cook, stirring, 1 minute. Gradually whisk in stock and milk; continue cooking until thickened. Season to taste with pepper. Use as is, or purée in food processor or blender.

PER 2 TBSP (25 mL)	
Calories	12
Protein	1 g
Fat, total	1 g
Fat, saturated	0.4 g
Carbohydrates	1 g
Sodium	10 mg
Cholesterol	4 mg
Fiber	0 g

Hoisin Barbecue Sauce

**MAKES 3/4 CUP
(175 mL)**

1/3 cup	hoisin sauce	75 mL
3 tbsp	soya sauce	45 mL
2 tbsp	ketchup	25 mL
2 tbsp	packed brown sugar	25 mL
2 tbsp	rice wine vinegar	25 mL
2 tsp	minced garlic	10 mL

1. In a small bowl, whisk together hoisin sauce, soya sauce, ketchup, brown sugar, vinegar and garlic.

TIP

This sauce is great as a marinade for tofu.

Use over grilled vegetables.

Try this sauce over rice or other grains.

MAKE AHEAD

Prepare up to 4 days in advance.

PER TBSP (15 mL)

Calories	27
Protein	1 g
Fat, total	0 g
Fat, saturated	0.0 g
Carbohydrates	6 g
Sodium	427 mg
Cholesterol	0 mg
Fiber	0 g

TOMATO, POTATO AND ARTICHOKE SALAD WITH ORIENTAL DRESSING (PAGE 87) ➤
OVERLEAF: ORIENTAL VEGETABLE SALAD (PAGE 80)

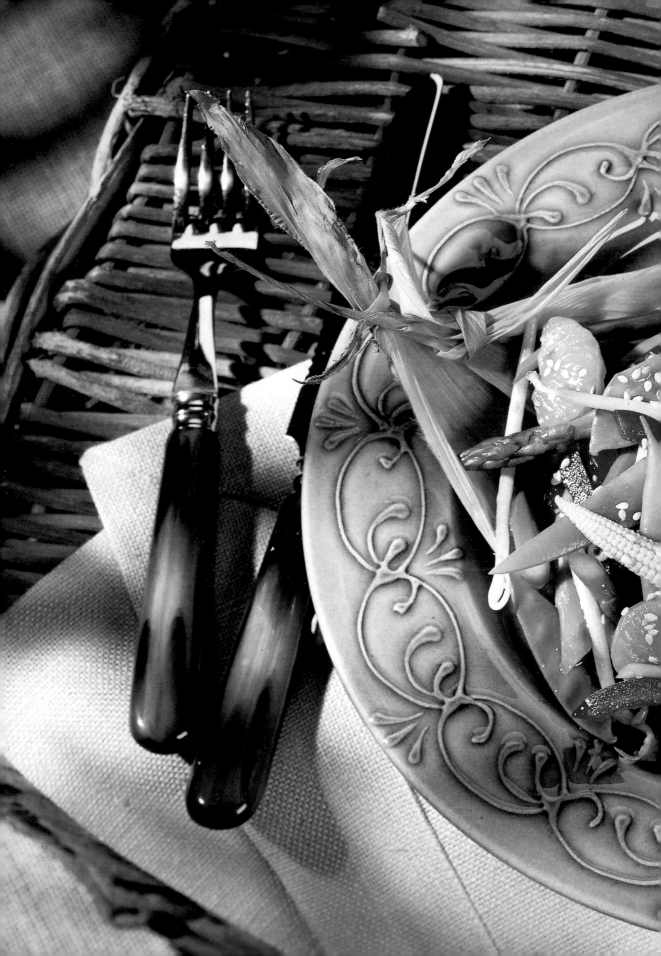

Honey Orange Poppy Seed Dressing

MAKES 1/3 CUP (75 mL)

TIP

Canola oil is the best vegetable oil to use in this recipe.

Serve over fruit salads or delicate lettuces such as Bibb.

MAKE AHEAD

Prepare up to 2 days in advance.

3 tbsp	vegetable oil (see Tip, at left)	45 mL
1 tbsp	freshly squeezed lime juice *or* lemon juice	15 mL
1 tbsp	honey	15 mL
1 tbsp	water	15 mL
1 tsp	poppy seeds	5 mL
1 tsp	grated orange zest	5 mL

1. In a small bowl, whisk together oil, lime juice, honey, water, poppy seeds and orange zest.

PER TBSP (15 mL)

Calories	82
Protein	0 g
Fat, total	8 g
Fat, saturated	1.0 g
Carbohydrates	3 g
Sodium	0 mg
Cholesterol	0 mg
Fiber	0 g

≺ BEAN AND SWEET POTATO CHILI ON GARLIC POLENTA (PAGE 106)

Lemon, Feta Cheese and Oregano Dressing

TIP

Naturally a great dressing
on Greek salads.

Also wonderful on
steamed vegetables,
especially asparagus
and broccoli.

MAKE AHEAD

Prepare up to 2 days
in advance. Stir well
before serving.

3 tbsp	crumbled feta cheese (about 3/4 oz [20 g])	45 mL
3 tbsp	olive oil	45 mL
1 tbsp	freshly squeezed lemon juice	15 mL
2 tbsp	water	25 mL
3/4 tsp	dried oregano	4 mL
3/4 tsp	minced garlic	4 mL

1. In a small bowl, whisk together feta, olive oil, lemon juice, water, oregano and garlic.

PER TBSP (15 mL)	
Calories	69
Protein	1 g
Fat, total	7 g
Fat, saturated	2 g
Carbohydrates	1 g
Sodium	75 mg
Cholesterol	6 mg
Fiber	0 g

Oriental Ginger Sauce

TIP

Serve over stir-fried vegetables and cooked rice noodles for a quick meal.

Pour over steamed vegetables, hot or cold.

MAKE AHEAD

Prepare up to 2 days in advance. Add more stock if too thick.

3/4 cup	BASIC VEGETABLE STOCK (see recipe, page 36)	175 mL
3 tbsp	packed brown sugar	45 mL
2 tbsp	soya sauce	25 mL
2 tbsp	rice wine vinegar	25 mL
1 tbsp	cornstarch	15 mL
1 1/2 tsp	minced garlic	7 mL
1 tsp	sesame oil	5 mL
1 tsp	minced ginger root	5 mL

1. In a small saucepan, whisk together stock, brown sugar, soya sauce, vinegar, cornstarch, garlic, sesame oil and ginger. Cook over medium heat, stirring, until bubbly and thickened.

PER TBSP (15 mL)	
Calories	12
Protein	0 g
Fat, total	0 g
Fat, saturated	0 g
Carbohydrates	3 g
Sodium	110 mg
Cholesterol	0 mg
Fiber	0 g

Creamy Pesto Sauce

**MAKES 2/3 CUP
(150 mL)**

TIP

I used to make a light pesto without sour cream or margarine. But I find the creamy texture in this recipe is lovely over pasta, rice, pizzas or vegetables.

Use this sauce in recipes that call for pesto. You can use the store-bought variety, but it is much higher in fat and calories.

MAKE AHEAD

Prepare up to 3 days in advance or freeze up to 3 weeks.

1 cup	packed fresh basil	250 mL
1/4 cup	light sour cream	50 mL
2 tbsp	light mayonnaise	25 mL
1 1/2 tbsp	grated Parmesan cheese	22 mL
1 tbsp	olive oil	15 mL
1 tbsp	toasted pine nuts	15 mL
1 1/2 tsp	freshly squeezed lemon juice	7 mL
1 tsp	minced garlic	5 mL

1. In a food processor, combine basil, sour cream, mayonnaise, Parmesan, oil, pine nuts, lemon juice and garlic; process until smooth.

PER TBSP (15 mL)

Calories	33
Protein	1 g
Fat, total	3 g
Fat, saturated	1.0 g
Carbohydrates	1 g
Sodium	39 mg
Cholesterol	1 mg
Fiber	0 g

Fresh Plum Tomato Pesto

**MAKES 2 CUPS
(250 mL)**

TIP

Serve over hot pasta, rice or other grains.

Also great as a salsa with crackers or tortilla chips.

For a more pronounced basil flavor, use all basil and no parsley.

MAKE AHEAD

Prepare up to 1 day in advance.

12 oz	plum tomatoes (about 5), seeded	375 g
1 1/4 cups	packed fresh basil	300 mL
1/4 cup	packed fresh parsley	50 mL
3 tbsp	grated Parmesan cheese	45 mL
2 tbsp	olive oil	25 mL
2 tbsp	toasted pine nuts	25 mL
2 tsp	minced garlic	10 mL
1/2 tsp	chili powder	2 mL

1. In a food processor combine tomatoes, basil, parsley, Parmesan, olive oil, pine nuts, garlic and chili powder; process just until chunky.

PER TBSP (15 mL)	
Calories	16
Protein	1 g
Fat, total	1 g
Fat, saturated	0.3 g
Carbohydrates	1 g
Sodium	14 mg
Cholesterol	1 mg
Fiber	0 g

Sun-Dried Tomato Dressing

TIP

Use this versatile dressing over salad, vegetables, pasta, rice (or other grains) or as a topping for pizza.

To soften sun-dried tomatoes, pour boiling water over them and soak 15 minutes. Drain and chop.

MAKE AHEAD

Prepare up to 3 days in advance or freeze up to 4 weeks.

1/2 cup	chopped softened sun-dried tomatoes (see Tip, at left)	125 mL
1/4 cup	packed fresh basil	50 mL
1/4 cup	light sour cream	50 mL
2 tbsp	light mayonnaise	25 mL
1 1/2 tbsp	grated Parmesan cheese	22 mL
1 tbsp	toasted pine nuts	15 mL
1 tsp	minced garlic	5 mL
1/2 cup	BASIC VEGETABLE STOCK (see recipe, page 36) *or* water	125 mL

1. In a food processor combine sun-dried tomatoes, basil, sour cream, mayonnaise, Parmesan, pine nuts and garlic; purée until well mixed. With motor running, add stock through feed tube; process until smooth.

PER TBSP (15 mL)	
Calories	17
Protein	1 g
Fat, total	1 g
Fat, saturated	0.1 g
Carbohydrates	2 g
Sodium	59 mg
Cholesterol	1 mg
Fiber	0 g

Thai Lime Dressing

TIP

Serve over salad, stir-fried vegetables or rice noodles.

Also great over steamed vegetables.

On non-vegetarian days use over fish or chicken.

MAKE AHEAD

Prepare up to 3 days in advance. Stir before using.

3 tbsp	chopped fresh coriander	45 mL
2 tbsp	vegetable oil	25 mL
2 tbsp	freshly squeezed lime juice	25 mL
2 tbsp	peanut butter	25 mL
1 tbsp	rice wine vinegar	15 mL
1 tbsp	packed brown sugar	15 mL
1 tsp	sesame oil	5 mL
1/2 tsp	minced garlic	2 mL
1/2 tsp	minced ginger root	2 mL
1	green onion, chopped	1

1. In a food processor combine coriander, oil, lime juice, peanut butter, vinegar, brown sugar, sesame oil, garlic, ginger and green onion; process until smooth.

PER TBSP (15 mL)	
Calories	57
Protein	1 g
Fat, total	5 g
Fat, saturated	1 g
Carbohydrates	3 g
Sodium	17 mg
Cholesterol	0 mg
Fiber	0 g

Tomato Basil Dressing

TIP

Tastes like a creamy fresh tomato dressing.

Wonderful over soft lettuce leaves.

Delicious over sautéed zucchini or green beans.

MAKE AHEAD

Prepare up to 2 days in advance. Stir well before using.

3 tbsp	vegetable oil	45 mL
3 tbsp	water	45 mL
2 tbsp	tomato paste	25 mL
1 tbsp	minced fresh basil (or 1 tsp [5 mL] dried)	15 mL
1 tbsp	balsamic or red wine vinegar	15 mL
1 tbsp	freshly squeezed lemon juice	15 mL
2 1/2 tsp	honey	12 mL
1 tsp	minced garlic	5 mL

1. In a food processor combine oil, water, tomato paste, basil, vinegar, lemon juice, honey and garlic; purée until smooth.

PER TBSP (15 mL)

Calories	61
Protein	0 g
Fat, total	6 g
Fat, saturated	0.4 g
Carbohydrates	3 g
Sodium	3 mg
Cholesterol	0 mg
Fiber	0 g

Parsley Dressing

TIP

Serve over sliced tomatoes or use as a sandwich spread.

Great with vegetables.

On non-vegetarian days, use as a topping over fish or chicken.

Use as a parsley pesto over pasta.

MAKE AHEAD

Prepare up to 2 days in advance.

1 cup	packed fresh parsley	250 mL
1/2 cup	light sour cream	125 mL
1 tbsp	light mayonnaise	15 mL
1 tbsp	freshly squeezed lemon juice	15 mL
1 tsp	minced garlic	5 mL

1. In a food processor combine parsley, sour cream, mayonnaise, lemon juice and garlic; process until smooth.

PER TBSP (15 mL)

Calories	13
Protein	1 g
Fat, total	1 g
Fat, saturated	0.1 g
Carbohydrates	2 g
Sodium	16 mg
Cholesterol	0 mg
Fiber	0 g

Toasted Sesame Dressing

TIP

Great over steamed vegetables, especially green beans and broccoli.

Use for a stir-fry sauce.

Marinate tofu in this dressing and sauté with vegetables.

MAKE AHEAD

Prepare up to 3 days in advance.

2 tbsp	rice wine vinegar	25 mL
2 tbsp	packed brown sugar	25 mL
1 tbsp	water	15 mL
1 tbsp	sesame oil	15 mL
1 tbsp	vegetable oil	15 mL
1 tbsp	soya sauce	15 mL
2 tsp	toasted sesame seeds	10 mL
1/2 tsp	minced garlic	2 mL
1/4 tsp	minced ginger root	1 mL

1. In a small bowl, whisk together vinegar, brown sugar, water, sesame oil, vegetable oil, soya sauce, sesame seeds, garlic and ginger.

PER TBSP (15 mL)	
Calories	48
Protein	0 g
Fat, total	4 g
Fat, saturated	1.0 g
Carbohydrates	3 g
Sodium	131 mg
Cholesterol	0 mg
Fiber	0 g

SALADS

Asian Tabbouleh Salad with Soya Orange Dressing

SERVES 4 TO 6

TIP

Bulgur wheat can often be found in grocery stores next to the rice and other grains. If not, health food stores always carry it.

Bulgur can be replaced with couscous or quinoa.

Coriander can be replaced with basil, parsley or dill.

This salad is a great source of fiber.

MAKE AHEAD

Prepare early in the day. Dressing can be poured over early, allowing salad to marinate.

PER SERVING (6)

Calories	200
Protein	7 g
Fat, total	3 g
Fat, saturated	0.4 g
Carbohydrates	41 g
Sodium	131 mg
Cholesterol	0 mg
Fiber	9 g

Salad

2 cups	BASIC VEGETABLE STOCK (see recipe, page 36) *or* water	500 mL
1 1/2 cups	bulgur wheat	375 mL
1 cup	finely chopped red bell peppers	250 mL
1 cup	finely chopped water chestnuts	250 mL
1/2 cup	finely chopped green onions	125 mL
1/3 cup	chopped fresh coriander	75 mL
1 cup	broccoli florets	250 mL
1 cup	chopped snow peas	250 mL

Dressing

4 tsp	orange juice concentrate	20 mL
4 tsp	honey	20 mL
2 1/2 tsp	sesame oil	12 mL
2 1/2 tsp	soya sauce	12 mL
1 tsp	minced garlic	5 mL
1 tsp	freshly squeezed lemon juice	5 mL
3/4 tsp	minced ginger root	4 mL

1. In a saucepan bring stock or water to a boil. Stir in bulgur, cover and turn heat off. Let stand 15 minutes; drain, rinse with cold water and place in a serving bowl. Stir in red peppers, water chestnuts, green onions and coriander.

2. Boil or steam broccoli florets and snow peas 2 minutes or until tender-crisp. Rinse under cold water, drain and add to bulgur mixture.

3. Make the dressing: In a small bowl, whisk together orange juice concentrate, honey, sesame oil, soya sauce, garlic, lemon juice and ginger. Pour over bulgur mixture and toss to coat. Serve chilled or at room temperature.

Broccoli, Apricot and Red Pepper Salad in a Creamy Dressing

SERVES 4 TO 6

TIP

The vegetables and dried fruit give this salad a wonderful flavor and texture.

Use any dried fruits.

Substitute coriander, basil or parsley for the dill.

MAKE AHEAD

Prepare early in the day. Best served chilled.

4 cups	broccoli florets	1 L
1 cup	chopped carrots	250 mL
1 cup	sliced red bell peppers	250 mL
3/4 cup	sliced water chestnuts	175 mL
1/2 cup	chopped red onions	125 mL
1/2 cup	chopped dried apricots *or* dates	125 mL
1/3 cup	raisins	75 mL
2 oz	feta cheese, crumbled	50 g

Dressing

1/4 cup	chopped fresh dill	50 mL
1/4 cup	light mayonnaise	50 mL
1/4 cup	light sour cream	50 mL
2 tbsp	freshly squeezed lemon juice	25 mL
1 1/2 tsp	minced garlic	7 mL
	Freshly ground black pepper, to taste	

1. Boil or steam broccoli 3 minutes or until tender-crisp; drain. Rinse under cold water; drain well.

2. In a large serving bowl, combine broccoli, carrots, red peppers, water chestnuts, red onions, apricots, raisins and feta cheese.

3. In a small bowl, whisk together dill, mayonnaise, sour cream, lemon juice and garlic. Pour over salad; toss to coat. Season to taste with pepper.

PER SERVING (6)	
Calories	156
Protein	5 g
Fat, total	5 g
Fat, saturated	2 g
Carbohydrates	27 g
Sodium	184 mg
Cholesterol	8 mg
Fiber	4 g

Baby Corn, Broccoli and Cauliflower Salad in a Creamy Citrus Dressing

TIP

For the best flavor, be sure to use fresh citrus juices. Bottled juice concentrates tend to be more acidic.

1 tsp (5 mL) chili powder can replace jalapeno peppers.

Replace coriander with fresh dill or basil.

MAKE AHEAD

Prepare salad up to 1 day in advance. The salad will marinate.

PER SERVING (8)	
Calories	102
Protein	3 g
Fat, total	6 g
Fat, saturated	1 g
Carbohydrates	11 g
Sodium	460 mg
Cholesterol	0 mg
Fiber	2 g

Salad

2 cups	broccoli florets	500 mL
2 cups	cauliflower florets	500 mL
2 cups	chopped baby corn cobs	500 mL
2 cups	chopped red bell peppers	500 mL
1 cup	chopped water chestnuts	250 mL
3/4 cup	chopped green onions	175 mL

Dressing

1/3 cup	chopped fresh coriander	75 mL
3 tbsp	olive oil	45 mL
3 tbsp	light sour cream	45 mL
2 tbsp	freshly squeezed lemon juice	25 mL
2 tbsp	freshly squeezed lime juice	25 mL
2 tbsp	light mayonnaise	25 mL
2 tsp	honey	10 mL
1 1/2 tsp	minced garlic	7 mL
1 to 2 tsp	minced fresh jalapeno peppers	5 to 10 mL

1. Boil or steam broccoli and cauliflower 5 minutes or until tender-crisp. Rinse under cold water and drain. Put in a serving bowl.

2. Stir baby corn, red peppers, water chestnuts and green onions into broccoli-cauliflower mixture.

3. Make the dressing: In a small bowl, whisk together coriander, olive oil, sour cream, lemon juice, lime juice, mayonnaise, honey, garlic and jalapeno peppers. Pour over salad; toss to coat. Chill and serve.

Cold Oriental Noodles with Sesame Dressing

◆■◆■◆■ ◀━━━▶ ■◆■◆■◆

Dressing

1/4 cup	BASIC VEGETABLE STOCK (see recipe, page 36)	50 mL
3 tbsp	honey	45 mL
2 tbsp	tahini	25 mL
1 tbsp	rice wine vinegar	15 mL
1 tbsp	sesame oil	15 mL
1 tbsp	soya sauce	15 mL
1 1/2 tsp	toasted sesame seeds	7 mL
1 tsp	minced garlic	5 mL
1 tsp	minced ginger root	5 mL

Salad

8 oz	medium-size rice noodles	250 g
1 cup	asparagus cut in 1/2-inch (1 cm) pieces	250 ml
1 cup	chopped broccoli	250 mL
1 cup	chopped red bell peppers	250 mL
1/2 cup	chopped green onions	125 mL
1/3 cup	chopped fresh coriander	75 mL

1. In a food processor or blender, purée stock, honey, tahini, vinegar, sesame oil, soya sauce, sesame seeds, garlic and ginger. Set aside.

2. Pour boiling water over noodles to cover; soak 15 minutes or until soft. Drain; rinse with cold water and put in serving bowl.

3. Boil or steam asparagus and broccoli, about 1 minute or until tender-crisp. Rinse under cold water, drain and add to noodles. Add red peppers, green onions and coriander.

4. Pour dressing over noodles and vegetables; toss to coat.

Oriental Vegetable Salad

2 1/2 cups	trimmed green beans	625 mL
2 cups	asparagus cut into 1-inch (2.5 cm) pieces	500 mL
1 1/2 cups	halved snow peas	375 mL
1 3/4 cups	bean sprouts	425 mL
1 1/2 cups	sliced red bell peppers	375 mL
1 cup	chopped baby corn cobs	250 mL
3/4 cup	canned sliced water chestnuts, drained	175 mL
3/4 cup	canned mandarin oranges, drained	175 mL

Dressing

4 tsp	soya sauce	20 mL
4 tsp	rice wine vinegar	20 mL
1 tbsp	olive oil	15 mL
1 tbsp	honey	15 mL
2 tsp	sesame oil	10 mL
2 tsp	toasted sesame seeds	10 mL
1 1/2 tsp	minced garlic	7 mL
1 tsp	minced ginger root	5 mL

1. Boil or steam green beans and asparagus for 2 to 3 minutes or until tender-crisp; drain. Rinse under cold water and drain; transfer to a large serving bowl.

2. Boil or steam snow peas 45 seconds or until tender-crisp; drain. Rinse under cold water and drain; add to serving bowl along with bean sprouts, red peppers, corn cobs, water chestnuts and mandarin oranges. Toss to combine.

3. In a small bowl, whisk together soya sauce, vinegar, olive oil, honey, sesame oil, sesame seeds, garlic and ginger. Pour over salad; toss to coat.

Orzo Yellow Split-Pea Salad

TIP

Prepare vegetables while split peas are cooking.

Green split peas can replace yellow, although the salad will not have as sweet a taste.

Orzo is a rice-shaped pasta. If unavailable, use small shell pasta.

MAKE AHEAD

Prepare salad early in the day and toss. The salad will marinate.

Salad

3 cups	BASIC VEGETABLE STOCK (see recipe, page 36)	750 mL
3/4 cup	dried yellow split peas	175 mL
3/4 cup	orzo	175 mL
2 cups	asparagus, cut into 1-inch (2.5 cm) pieces	500 mL
1 cup	chopped baby corn cobs	250 mL
1 cup	chopped red bell peppers	250 mL
1 cup	chopped water chestnuts	250 mL
1/2 cup	chopped green onions	125 mL

Dressing

3 tbsp	rice wine vinegar	45 mL
3 tbsp	soya sauce	45 mL
4 tsp	sesame oil	20 mL
1 1/2 tsp	minced garlic	7 mL
1 1/2 tsp	minced ginger root	7 mL

1. In a saucepan bring stock to a boil. Stir in split peas, reduce heat to medium, cover and cook 25 to 30 minutes or until tender. Drain, rinse under cold water and place in a serving bowl.

2. In a pot of boiling water, cook orzo 8 to 10 minutes or until tender but firm. Rinse under cold water, drain and add to split peas.

3. Boil or steam asparagus 3 minutes or until tender-crisp. Rinse under cold water, drain and add to serving bowl along with baby corn, red peppers, water chestnuts and green onions.

4. Make the dressing: In a small bowl, whisk together vinegar, soya sauce, sesame oil, garlic and ginger.

5. Pour dressing over salad; toss to coat.

PER SERVING (8)

Calories	137
Protein	8 g
Fat, total	3 g
Fat, saturated	0.4 g
Carbohydrates	22 g
Sodium	539 mg
Cholesterol	0 mg
Fiber	2 g

Pear, Lettuce and Feta Cheese Salad

TIP

Sweet fruit and a combination of lettuces make this a perfect salad.

Any ripe fruit can replace pears.

If you don't care for the bitter flavor of curly endive and radicchio, use romaine or Bibb lettuce instead.

If you don't want the salad to wilt, use a larger amount of romaine lettuce.

MAKE AHEAD

Prepare salad and dressing early in the day. Toss just before serving.

Dressing

2 tbsp	raspberry vinegar	25 mL
2 1/2 tbsp	olive oil	35 mL
1 tsp	minced garlic	5 mL
1 1/2 tsp	honey	7 mL
1 tsp	sesame oil	5 mL

Salad

4 cups	red or green leaf lettuce, washed, dried and torn into pieces	1 L
1 1/2 cups	curly endive or escarole, washed, dried and torn into pieces	375 mL
1 1/2 cups	radicchio, washed, dried and torn into pieces	375 mL
1 cup	diced pears (about 1 pear)	250 mL
2 oz	feta cheese, crumbled	50 g
1/3 cup	sliced black olives	75 mL

1. Prepare the dressing: In a small bowl, whisk together vinegar, olive oil, garlic, honey and sesame oil; set aside.

2. Make the salad: In a serving bowl, combine leaf lettuce, curly endive, radicchio, pears, feta and olives. Pour dressing over; toss gently to coat. Serve immediately.

PER SERVING (6)

Calories	108
Protein	2 g
Fat, total	8 g
Fat, saturated	2 g
Carbohydrates	8 g
Sodium	165 mg
Cholesterol	8 mg
Fiber	2 g

Potato Salad with Goat Cheese Dressing

SERVES 4 TO 6

TIP

Yukon Gold potatoes provide a sweeter, richer taste than regular potatoes and have a firmer texture. They are readily available.

Try feta instead of goat cheese.

This is great potato salad to serve at any time of the year.

MAKE AHEAD

Prepare up to 1 day in advance.

PER SERVING (6)

Calories	222
Protein	8 g
Fat, total	5 g
Fat, saturated	0.2 g
Carbohydrates	37 g
Sodium	121 mg
Cholesterol	0 mg
Fiber	4 g

Salad

2 lbs	Yukon Gold potatoes	1 kg
1 cup	chopped red bell peppers	250 mL
3/4 cup	chopped fresh coriander	175 mL
1/2 cup	chopped green onions	125 mL
1 cup	chopped carrots	250 mL
1 cup	halved snow peas	250 mL

Dressing

4 oz	goat cheese	125 g
3 tbsp	light sour cream	45 mL
2 tbsp	light mayonnaise	25 mL
3 tbsp	freshly squeezed lemon juice	45 mL
1 tsp	minced garlic	5 mL
1/2 tsp	freshly ground black pepper	2 mL
1/4 cup	water *or* vegetable stock	50 mL

1. Scrub but do not peel potatoes; cut into large chunks. Put in a saucepan; add cold water to cover. Bring to a boil; reduce heat to simmer and cook about 15 minutes or until tender when pierced with tip of knife. Rinse under cold water and drain; put in a serving bowl along with red peppers, coriander and green onions.

2. In a small saucepan, add cold water to cover carrots. Bring to a boil. Reduce heat to simmer; cook 4 minutes or until tender. Drain; add to serving bowl.

3. Boil or steam snow peas 45 seconds or until tender-crisp. Rinse under cold water, drain and add to serving bowl.

4. Dressing: In a small bowl, stir together goat cheese, sour cream, mayonnaise, lemon juice, garlic and pepper until smooth. Add water to thin dressing.

5. Pour dressing over salad and toss to coat. Serve immediately, or chill and serve cold.

Split-Pea and Rice Greek Salad

◆■◆■◆■◆■◆▶ ▮◆■◆■◆■◆

4 1/2 cups	BASIC VEGETABLE STOCK (see recipe, page 36)	1.125 L
1 cup	dried green split peas	250 mL
1 cup	white or brown rice	250 mL
1 1/2 cups	chopped tomatoes	375 mL
1 cup	chopped unpeeled cucumbers	250 mL
1 cup	chopped red bell peppers	250 mL
3/4 cup	chopped red onions	175 mL
1/3 cup	sliced black olives	75 mL
3 oz	feta cheese, crumbled	75 g

Dressing

2 tbsp	freshly squeezed lemon juice	25 mL
1 1/2 tbsp	olive oil	20 mL
1 tbsp	balsamic vinegar	15 mL
1 1/2 tsp	minced garlic	7 mL
1 1/2 tsp	dried oregano	7 mL
1/2 tsp	coarsely ground black pepper	2 mL

1. In a saucepan bring 3 cups (750 mL) of the stock to a boil. Stir in split peas; reduce heat to medium and cook, covered, 25 to 35 minutes or until tender. Rinse under cold water and drain; set aside to cool.

2. Meanwhile, in a saucepan bring remaining 1 1/2 cups (375 mL) stock to a boil. Stir in rice; reduce heat to low, cover and cook 20 minutes or until rice is tender and stock absorbed. (Brown rice will need 35 minutes and a little more stock.) Set aside to cool.

3. In a large serving bowl, combine tomatoes, cucumbers, red peppers, onions, olives, feta and cooled rice and split peas.

4. Make the dressing: In a small bowl, whisk together lemon juice, olive oil, balsamic vinegar, garlic, oregano and pepper. Pour over salad; toss to coat.

SERVES 6

TIP

Split peas and rice are a dynamic combination.

This is a great variation of traditional Greek salad.

Add other vegetables of your choice.

MAKE AHEAD

Prepare early in the day.

PER SERVING

Calories	338
Protein	14 g
Fat, total	7 g
Fat, saturated	2.6 g
Carbohydrates	55 g
Sodium	227 mg
Cholesterol	12 mg
Fiber	3 g

Tomatoes Stuffed with Corn, Black Beans and Pine Nuts

TIP

These stuffed tomatoes are visually stunning. Serve as an appetizer or a side vegetable dish.

If black beans are unavailable, use chick peas or white navy beans.

The filling is great as a salad by itself.

MAKE AHEAD

Prepare filling up to 1 day in advance. Stuff tomatoes a few hours before serving.

4	medium tomatoes	4
1/2 cup	canned corn kernels, drained	125 mL
1/2 cup	canned black beans, rinsed and drained	125 mL
1/4 cup	chopped fresh coriander	50 mL
1/4 cup	chopped green onions	50 mL
1/4 cup	chopped red bell peppers	50 mL
2 tbsp	light mayonnaise	25 mL
2 tbsp	toasted pine nuts	25 mL
1 tbsp	grated Parmesan cheese	15 mL
2 tsp	freshly squeezed lemon juice	10 mL
1 tsp	Dijon mustard	5 mL

1. Slice tops off tomatoes and reserve. Scoop out and discard seeds and core.

2. In a small bowl, mix together corn, black beans, coriander, green onions, red peppers, mayonnaise, pine nuts, Parmesan, lemon juice and Dijon.

3. Divide mixture evenly between tomato shells, about 1/3 cup (75 mL) per tomato. Cover with reserved tomato tops and serve.

PER SERVING

Calories	136
Protein	6 g
Fat, total	6 g
Fat, saturated	1 g
Carbohydrates	19 g
Sodium	238 mg
Cholesterol	1 mg
Fiber	5 g

Tortilla Bean Salad with Creamy Salsa Dressing

SERVES 4

TIP

Southwestern all the way, this salad is low in fat — thanks to the light dressing.

Use a mild or hot salsa, whichever you prefer.

Vary beans and vegetables to your taste.

To prevent salad from wilting, do not pour dressing over until ready to serve.

MAKE AHEAD

Prepare salad and dressing early in the day. Toss just before serving.

PER SERVING

Calories	263
Protein	11 g
Fat, total	7 g
Fat, saturated	1 g
Carbohydrates	42 g
Sodium	443 mg
Cholesterol	1 mg
Fiber	10 g

Salad

3 cups	romaine lettuce, washed, dried and torn into pieces	750 mL
1 cup	canned chickpeas, rinsed and drained	250 mL
1 cup	canned red kidney beans rinsed and drained	250 mL
1 cup	shredded carrots	250 mL
1 cup	chopped red bell peppers	250 mL
3/4 cup	chopped red onions	175 mL
1/3 cup	chopped fresh coriander	75 mL

Dressing

3 tbsp	salsa	45 mL
3 tbsp	light sour cream	45 mL
2 tbsp	light mayonnaise	25 mL
1 tsp	minced garlic	5 mL
3/4 to 1 tsp	chili powder	4 to 5 mL
1 oz	tortilla chips, crushed (about 12)	25 g

1. In a large bowl, combine lettuce, chickpeas, kidney beans, carrots, red peppers, red onions and coriander.

2. Make the dressing: In a small bowl, whisk together salsa, sour cream, mayonnaise, garlic and chili powder.

3. Just before serving, pour dressing over salad. Toss to coat. Sprinkle with tortilla chips. Serve immediately.

Tomato, Potato and Artichoke Salad with Oriental Dressing

◆■◆■◆■◄███►■◆■◆■◆

1 lb	red potatoes (about 3)	500 g
3	plum tomatoes, seeded	3
1	can (14 oz [398 mL]) artichoke hearts, drained and quartered	1
3/4 cup	chopped red onions	175 mL
1/2 cup	chopped fresh coriander	125 mL
1/3 cup	chopped green onions	75 mL

Dressing

2 tbsp	rice wine vinegar	25 mL
2 tbsp	soya sauce	25 mL
1 tbsp	sesame oil	15 mL
1 tbsp	vegetable oil	15 mL
1 tbsp	honey	15 mL
1 tsp	minced garlic	5 mL
1 tsp	minced ginger root	5 mL

1. Scrub but do not peel potatoes; cut into 1 1/2 inch (4 cm) pieces and put in a saucepan. Add cold water to cover; bring to a boil, reduce heat to simmer and cook until tender, about 15 minutes. Rinse under cold water and drain.

2. Cut tomatoes into 1 1/2 inch (4 cm) pieces. In a serving bowl, combine potatoes, tomatoes, artichokes, red onions, coriander and green onions.

3. Make the dressing: In a small bowl, whisk together vinegar, soya sauce, sesame oil, vegetable oil, honey, garlic and ginger. Just before serving, pour over salad; toss to coat.

Three-Tomato Salad with Goat Cheese Dressing

TIP

Tomatoes and goat cheese are a great combination.

To soften sun-dried tomatoes, cover with boiling water and let soak 15 minutes; drain and chop.

If yellow tomatoes are available, use them instead of regular tomatoes.

MAKE AHEAD

Prepare salad and dressing early in the day. Toss just before serving.

Dressing

3 oz	goat cheese	75 g
1/4 cup	light sour cream	50 mL
3 tbsp	light mayonnaise	45 mL
1 1/2 tsp	dried basil	7 mL
1 tsp	minced garlic	5 mL

Salad

3 cups	chopped tomatoes (about 1 lb [500 g])	750 mL
3 cups	quartered plum tomatoes (about 1 lb [500 g])	750 mL
1 cup	chopped softened sun-dried tomatoes (see Tip, at left)	250 mL

1. In a food processor, purée goat cheese, sour cream, mayonnaise, basil and garlic until smooth, scraping down sides of bowl once or twice.

2. In a serving bowl, combine tomatoes, plum tomatoes and sun-dried tomatoes.

3. Pour dressing over salad; toss to coat.

PER SERVING (6)

Calories	114
Protein	5 g
Fat, total	5 g
Fat, saturated	0.3 g
Carbohydrates	15 g
Sodium	298 mg
Cholesterol	0 mg
Fiber	3 g

Vegetable Salad with Feta Dressing

◆■□◆□■□■□◆◆■□■□◆□■◆

Salad

2 cups	chopped celery	500 mL
2 cups	chopped English cucumbers	500 mL
2 cups	chopped red bell peppers	500 mL
2 cups	chopped plum tomatoes	500 mL
1 cup	chopped red onions	250 mL
1/3 cup	sliced black olives	75 mL

Dressing

2 oz	feta cheese, crumbled	50 g
1/3 cup	light sour cream	75 mL
2 tbsp	2% plain yogurt	25 mL
1 tbsp	freshly squeezed lemon juice	15 mL
1 1/2 tsp	minced garlic	7 mL
1 1/4 tsp	dried oregano	6 mL

1. In a serving bowl, combine celery, cucumbers, red peppers, tomatoes, red onions and olives.

2. Make the dressing: In a food processor or blender, combine feta, sour cream, yogurt, lemon juice, garlic and oregano; process until smooth.

3. Pour dressing over salad; toss to coat.

Warm Spinach and Mushroom Salad

◆■◆■◆■◆━━━━◆■◆■◆■◆

SERVES 4 TO 6

TIP

To soften sun-dried tomatoes, cover with boiling water and let soak for 15 minutes. Drain and chop.

Try this recipe with different mushrooms — such as cremini or, for a decadent evening, shiitake or chanterelles.

Common mushrooms will also work well with this recipe.

MAKE AHEAD

Prepare dressing and sauté mushroom mixture early in the day. Do not mix with salad. When ready to serve, reheat mushroom mixture and toss with dressing and salad.

Dressing

3 tbsp	balsamic vinegar	45 mL
4 tsp	olive oil	20 mL
1 tsp	minced garlic	5 mL

Salad

6 cups	washed, dried and torn spinach leaves	1.5 L
1/2 cup	chopped softened sun-dried tomatoes (see Tip, at left)	125 mL
1/4 cup	toasted chopped walnuts	50 mL
2 tsp	vegetable oil	10 mL
1 tsp	minced garlic	5 mL
2 cups	sliced oyster mushrooms	500 mL
3/4 cup	sliced red onions	175 mL

1. In a small bowl, whisk together vinegar, olive oil and garlic. Set aside.

2. Put spinach, sun-dried tomatoes and walnuts in a large serving bowl.

3. In a large nonstick frying pan, heat oil over high heat. Add garlic, mushrooms and red onions; cook 6 minutes, or until mushrooms are browned and any excess liquid is absorbed. Quickly add hot vegetables and dressing to spinach and toss. Serve immediately.

PER SERVING (6)

Calories	108
Protein	4 g
Fat, total	8 g
Fat, saturated	1 g
Carbohydrates	9 g
Sodium	143 mg
Cholesterol	0 mg
Fiber	3 g

Red-and-Green Coleslaw with Apricots and Fennel

TIP

Here's a great twist on traditional coleslaw, with the sweet flavors of apricots, fennel and balsamic vinegar.

Toast nuts in a nonstick skillet over high heat until browned, about 2 to 3 minutes.

MAKE AHEAD

Prepare up to 1 day in advance. Best if tossed just before serving.

Salad

3 cups	thinly sliced green cabbage	750 mL
3 cups	thinly sliced red cabbage	750 mL
1 1/2 cups	thinly sliced red bell peppers	375 mL
1 cup	chopped dried apricots	250 mL
1 cup	canned corn kernels, drained	250 mL
1 cup	thinly sliced fennel	250 mL
1/2 cup	chopped green onions	125 mL
1/4 cup	toasted slivered almonds	50 mL
2 tbsp	toasted sesame seeds	25 mL

Dressing

1/4 cup	balsamic vinegar	50 mL
3 tbsp	olive oil	45 mL
1 1/2 tsp	minced garlic	7 mL

1. In a large bowl, combine green cabbage, red cabbage, red peppers, apricots, corn, fennel, green onions, almonds and sesame seeds.

2. Make the dressing: In a small bowl, whisk together vinegar, oil and garlic.

3. Pour dressing over salad; toss to coat.

PER SERVING (6)	
Calories	219
Protein	5 g
Fat, total	11 g
Fat, saturated	1 g
Carbohydrates	31 g
Sodium	125 mg
Cholesterol	0 mg
Fiber	6 g

MAIN AND SIDE DISHES

Vermicelli Sesame Oriental Vegetable Wraps

TIP

Flavored tortillas — such as pesto, sun-dried tomato, herb or whole wheat — are now appearing in many supermarkets. Using different flavors will add taste variety and visual interest to these wraps.

Substitute other vegetables of your choice.

Fresh parsley or dill can replace coriander.

Any thin-strand pasta will work well.

MAKE AHEAD

Prepare filling up to 1 day in advance.

Tortillas are best filled just before serving, but can be filled 1 or 2 hours ahead.

PER SERVING

Calories	319
Protein	9 g
Fat, total	8 g
Fat, saturated	1.8 g
Carbohydrates	52 g
Sodium	594 mg
Cholesterol	0 mg
Fiber	3 g

2 tbsp	light mayonnaise	25 mL
4 tsp	soya sauce	20 mL
1 tbsp	water	15 mL
1 tbsp	sesame oil	15 mL
1 1/2 tsp	honey	7 mL
1 tsp	minced garlic	5 mL
3/4 tsp	minced ginger root	4 mL
1/4 cup	sliced carrots	50 mL
1/2 cup	halved snow peas	125 mL
1/3 cup	sliced baby corn cobs	75 mL
1/3 cup	chopped red or green bell peppers	75 mL
1/3 cup	chopped fresh coriander	75 mL
1	green onion, chopped	1
4 oz	vermicelli or capellini, broken into thirds	125 g
4	10-inch (25 cm) flour tortillas, preferably different flavors, if available	4

1. In a food processor, combine mayonnaise, soya sauce, water, sesame oil, honey, garlic and ginger; process until smooth. Set aside.

2. Boil or steam carrots 3 minutes or until tender-crisp; rinse with cold water, drain and put in serving bowl. Boil or steam snow peas for 1 minute or until tender-crisp; rinse with cold water, drain and add to serving bowl. Add baby corn, peppers, coriander and green onion.

3. In a large pot of boiling water, cook vermicelli 8 to 10 minutes until tender but firm. Drain and add to serving bowl. Add sauce; toss all ingredients until well mixed.

4. Divide pasta mixture between tortillas. Form each tortilla into a packet by folding bottom edge over filling, then sides, then top, to enclose filling completely.

Sun-Dried Tomato Pizza Wraps

Preheat oven to 400° F (200° C)

Baking sheet

4	10-inch (25 cm) flour tortillas, preferably different flavors, if available	4
1/2 cup	prepared tomato pasta sauce	125 mL
1/2 cup	diced red bell peppers	125 mL
1/3 cup	chopped green onions	75 mL
1/4 cup	chopped softened sun-dried tomatoes (see Tip, at left)	50 mL
1 cup	shredded part-skim mozzarella cheese (about 4 oz [125 g])	250 mL
2 oz	feta cheese, crumbled	50 g

1. Lay out a tortilla on work surface and spread with one-quarter of tomato sauce. Repeat with remaining tortillas.

2. In the center of each tortilla, sprinkle one-quarter of the red peppers, the green onions and the sun-dried tomatoes. Top with mozzarella and feta cheeses, divided equally between tortillas.

3. Form each tortilla into a packet by folding bottom edge over filling, then sides, then top, to enclose filling completely. Place packets seam-side down on baking sheet. Bake for 10 minutes or until hot.

Goat Cheese and Tomato Salad Wraps

TIP

Flavored tortillas — such as pesto, sun-dried tomato, herb or whole wheat — are now appearing in many supermarkets. Using different flavors will add taste variety and visual interest to these wraps.

Plum tomatoes provide a firmer texture and less excess liquid.

If 10-inch (25 cm) tortillas are unavailable, use a smaller size and make 6 wraps.

MAKE AHEAD

Prepare vegetables early in day, but don't combine until just before serving.

4 oz	goat cheese, crumbled	125 g
1 1/4 cups	diced seeded tomatoes	300 mL
1 1/4 cups	diced cucumbers	300 mL
1/2 cup	chopped green onions	125 mL
2 tsp	olive oil	10 mL
2 tsp	balsamic vinegar	10 mL
4	10-inch (25 cm) flour tortillas, preferably different flavors, if available	4

1. In a bowl combine goat cheese, tomatoes, cucumbers, green onions, oil and vinegar. Divide mixture equally between tortillas.

2. Form each tortilla into a packet by folding bottom edge over filling, then sides, then top, to enclose filling completely.

PER SERVING

Calories	276
Protein	10 g
Fat, total	14 g
Fat, saturated	1.5 g
Carbohydrates	28 g
Sodium	395 mg
Cholesterol	0 mg
Fiber	3 g

CARROT ROLL WITH ARTICHOKE GARLIC FILLING (PAGE 118) ➤

OVERLEAF: POTATO CRUST PESTO PIZZA (PAGE 126)

Hummus and Sautéed Vegetable Wraps

SERVES 4

TIP

Flavored tortillas — such as pesto, sun-dried tomato, herb or whole wheat — are now appearing in many supermarkets. The different colors make these wraps an attractive dish for entertaining.

Try substituting other herbs — such as coriander, basil or parsley — for the dill.

If tahini is unavailable, use peanut butter.

MAKE AHEAD

Prepare hummus up to 3 days in advance.

Sauté vegetables early in day and reheat before serving.

PER SERVING

Calories	383
Protein	11 g
Fat, total	17 g
Fat, saturated	2.9 g
Carbohydrates	48 g
Sodium	414 mg
Cholesterol	0 mg
Fiber	7 g

1 cup	canned chickpeas, rinsed and drained	250 mL
1/4 cup	tahini	50 mL
1/4 cup	water	50 mL
2 tbsp	freshly squeezed lemon juice	25 mL
4 tsp	olive oil	20 mL
1 tbsp	chopped fresh parsley	15 mL
3/4 tsp	minced garlic	4 mL
2 tsp	vegetable oil	10 mL
1 cup	diced onions	250 mL
1 1/4 cups	diced red bell peppers	300 mL
1 1/4 cups	chopped snow peas	300 mL
1/4 cup	chopped fresh dill (or 2 tsp [10 mL] dried)	50 mL
4	10-inch (25 cm) flour tortillas, preferably different flavors, if available	4

1. Make the hummus: In a food processor, combine chickpeas, tahini, water, lemon juice, oil, parsley and garlic; process until creamy and smooth. Transfer to a bowl and set aside

2. In a large nonstick saucepan, heat oil over medium-high heat. Add onions and sauté 4 minutes or until soft and browned. Add red peppers and sauté 4 minutes until soft. Add snow peas and sauté 2 minutes or until tender-crisp. Stir in dill and remove from heat.

3. Divide hummus equally among tortillas, spreading to within 1/2 inch (1 cm) of edge. Divide vegetable mixture between tortillas. Form each tortilla into a packet by folding bottom edge over filling, then sides, then top, to enclose filling completely.

< BLACK BEAN, CORN AND LEEK FRITTATA (PAGE 121)

Potato Parmesan with Tomato Sauce and Cheese

◆■◆■◆■□◀▶■◆■◆■◆■◆

SERVES 4 TO 6

TIP

Yukon gold potatoes are great in this recipe.

Fresh parsley or basil can replace dill.

Try this with eggplant or zucchini. Boil just until tender.

MAKE AHEAD

Cook potatoes up to 2 days in advance.

Prepare entire recipe 1 day in advance; bake just before serving.

Preheat oven to 350° F (180° C)

Baking sheet sprayed with vegetable spray

3	large potatoes, scrubbed but not peeled (about 1 lb [500 g])	3
1	egg	1
1	egg white	1
3 tbsp	2% milk *or* water	45 mL
1/2 cup	dry seasoned bread crumbs	125 mL
2 tbsp	chopped fresh dill (or 1/2 tsp [2 mL] dried)	25 mL
1 tbsp	grated Parmesan cheese	15 mL
3/4 cup	prepared tomato pasta sauce	175 mL
1/2 cup	shredded part-skim mozzarella cheese (about 2 oz [50 g])	125 mL

1. In a saucepan add cold water to cover to potatoes. Bring to a boil; cook 20 to 25 minutes or just until barely tender when pierced with a fork. Drain. When cool enough to handle, cut into 1/2-inch (1 cm) round slices (or rinse with cold water if in a hurry).

2. In small bowl, whisk together whole egg, egg white and milk.

3. On a plate stir together bread crumbs, dill and Parmesan.

4. Dip potato slices in egg wash, coat with crumb mixture and place on prepared baking sheet. Repeat with all potato slices.

5. Bake 15 minutes, turning at the halfway point, or until golden and tender when pierced with a fork. Top each slice with some tomato sauce and sprinkle with mozzarella; bake 5 minutes longer.

PER SERVING (6)	
Calories	174
Protein	8 g
Fat, total	5 g
Fat, saturated	2.0 g
Carbohydrates	26 g
Sodium	433 mg
Cholesterol	42 mg
Fiber	2 g

Bean Burgers with Dill Sauce

TIP

Serve in a pita or tortilla with lettuce, tomatoes and onions.

Another simple topping can be made with 3 parts 2% yogurt and 1 part Dijon mustard.

Substitute black beans with another bean of your choice.

MAKE AHEAD

Prepare mixture and sauce up to 1 day in advance. Reheat gently.

PER SERVING (9)

Calories	126
Protein	7 g
Fat, total	2 g
Fat, saturated	0.4 g
Carbohydrates	20 g
Sodium	262 mg
Cholesterol	27 mg
Fiber	5 g

Preheat oven to 425° F (220° C)
Baking sheet sprayed with vegetable spray

Burgers

2 cups	canned black beans, rinsed and drained	500 mL
1/2 cup	dry seasoned bread crumbs	125 mL
1/3 cup	chopped fresh dill	75 mL
1/3 cup	chopped red onions	75 mL
1/4 cup	finely chopped carrots	50 mL
2 tbsp	cornmeal	25 mL
1	egg	1
1 1/2 tsp	minced garlic	7 mL
1/4 tsp	salt	1 mL

Sauce

3 tbsp	light sour cream	45 mL
2 tbsp	light mayonnaise	25 mL
2 tsp	freshly squeezed lemon juice	10 mL
1/4 to 1/2 tsp	minced garlic	1 to 2 mL
1 tbsp	chopped fresh dill (or 1/2 tsp [2 mL] dried)	15 mL

1. In a food processor, combine black beans, bread crumbs, dill, onions, carrots, cornmeal, egg, garlic and salt. Pulse on and off until well combined. With wet hands, scoop up 1/4 cup (50 mL) of mixture and form into a patty. Put on prepared baking sheet. Repeat procedure for remaining patties.

2. Bake 15 minutes, turning at the halfway point.

3. Meanwhile, make the sauce: In a small bowl, stir together sour cream, mayonnaise, lemon juice, garlic and dill.

4. Serve burgers hot with sauce on side.

Zucchini Stuffed with Rice and Mushrooms

◆■◆■◆■◆◀▶■◆■◆■◆■◆

TIP

Wild rice can be replaced with brown or white rice or a combination. Cook white rice for only 15 to 20 minutes; allow 35 minutes for brown rice.

For a spicier version of this dish, try adding 1/2 tsp (2 mL) chili powder.

MAKE AHEAD

Prepare up to 1 day in advance and bake just before serving.

PER SERVING

Calories	135
Protein	6 g
Fat, total	2 g
Fat, saturated	0.2 g
Carbohydrates	27 g
Sodium	404 mg
Cholesterol	0 mg
Fiber	5 g

Preheat oven to 350° F (180° C)

13- by 9-inch (3 L) baking dish sprayed with vegetable spray

3 cups	BASIC VEGETABLE STOCK (see recipe, page 36)	750 mL
1/2 cup	wild rice	125 mL
2	large zucchini (each about 8 oz [250 g])	2
1 tsp	vegetable oil	5 mL
2 tsp	minced garlic	10 mL
3/4 cup	chopped onions	175 mL
2 cups	sliced mushrooms	500 mL
1 1/2 tsp	drained capers	7 mL
1 tsp	dried basil	5 mL
1/2 tsp	dried oregano	2 mL
3/4 cup	prepared tomato pasta sauce	175 mL
3 tbsp	grated Parmesan cheese (optional)	45 mL

1. In a small saucepan, bring stock to a boil; stir in rice, cover, reduce heat to low and cook 35 to 40 minutes or until rice is tender. Drain excess liquid.

2. Meanwhile, cut each zucchini in half lengthwise. In a large pot of boiling water, cook zucchini 4 minutes; drain. When cool enough to handle, carefully scoop out pulp, leaving shells intact. Chop pulp and set aside. Put zucchini shells into prepared baking dish.

3. In a large nonstick frying pan sprayed with vegetable spray, heat oil over medium-high heat. Add garlic and onions; cook 3 minutes or until softened. Stir in mushrooms, capers, basil and oregano; cook 5 minutes or until mushrooms are browned. Stir in zucchini pulp; cook 2 minutes. Remove from heat.

4. Stir cooked rice, tomato sauce and 1 tbsp (15 mL) of the Parmesan cheese, if desired, into vegetable mixture. Stuff mixture evenly into zucchini boats, mounding filling high. Sprinkle with remaining Parmesan, if desired. Cover dish tightly with foil.

5. Bake 15 minutes or until heated through.

Spicy Rice, Bean and Lentil Casserole

TIP

This makes an excellent total meal for vegetarians.

Instead of lentils, substitute green or yellow split peas.

Grilled or barbecued corn is excellent in this dish.

Any type of bean can replace the red kidney beans.

This dish is a great source of fiber.

MAKE AHEAD

Prepare up to 2 days in advance and reheat gently.

2 tsp	vegetable oil	10 mL
2 tsp	minced garlic	10 mL
1 cup	chopped onions	250 mL
3/4 cup	chopped green peppers	175 mL
3 3/4 cups	BASIC VEGETABLE STOCK (see recipe, page 36)	950 mL
3/4 cup	brown rice	175 mL
1/2 cup	green lentils	125 mL
1 tsp	dried basil	5 mL
1 tsp	chili powder	5 mL
1	can (19 oz [540 mL]) red kidney beans, rinsed and drained	1
1 cup	canned or frozen corn kernels, drained	250 mL
1 cup	medium salsa	250 mL

1. In a nonstick saucepan, heat oil over medium-high heat. Add garlic, onions and green peppers; cook 3 minutes. Stir in stock, brown rice, lentils, basil and chili powder; bring to a boil, cover, reduce heat to medium-low and cook 30 to 40 minutes, stirring occasionally, until rice and lentils are tender and liquid is absorbed.

2. Stir in beans, corn and salsa; cover and cook 5 minutes or until heated through.

PER SERVING (6)

Calories	278
Protein	14 g
Fat, total	3 g
Fat, saturated	0.4 g
Carbohydrates	52 g
Sodium	361 mg
Cholesterol	0 mg
Fiber	9 g

Chickpea Tofu Burgers with Coriander Mayonnaise

◆■□■□■□◆■■□■◆■◆

Preheat oven to 425° F (220° C)
Baking sheet sprayed with vegetable spray

1 cup	canned chickpeas, rinsed and drained	250 mL
8 oz	firm tofu	250 g
1/3 cup	dry bread crumbs	75 mL
2 tbsp	tahini	25 mL
1 1/2 tbsp	freshly squeezed lemon juice	20 mL
1 tsp	minced garlic	5 mL
1	egg	1
1/4 tsp	freshly ground black pepper	1 mL
1/4 tsp	salt	1 mL
1/3 cup	chopped fresh coriander	75 mL
1/4 cup	chopped green onions	50 mL
1/4 cup	chopped red bell peppers	50 mL

Sauce

1/4 cup	2% plain yogurt	50 mL
1/4 cup	light sour cream	50 mL
1/4 cup	chopped fresh coriander	50 mL
1 tbsp	light mayonnaise	15 mL
1/2 tsp	minced garlic	2 mL

1. In a food processor, combine chickpeas, tofu, bread crumbs, tahini, lemon juice, garlic, egg, pepper and salt; process until smooth. Add coriander, green onions and red peppers; pulse on and off until well-mixed. With wet hands, scoop up 1/4 cup (50 mL) of mixture and form into a patty. Put on prepared baking sheet. Repeat procedure for remaining patties. Bake 20 minutes, turning burgers at halfway point.

2. Meanwhile, make the sauce: In a small bowl, stir together yogurt, sour cream, coriander, mayonnaise and garlic; set aside.

3. Serve burgers hot with sauce on side.

SERVES 4 TO 5

TIP

Serve in pita breads or on rolls, with lettuce, tomatoes and onions.

Tofu is found in the vegetable section of your grocery store. If desired, it can be replaced with 5% ricotta cheese.

Tahini is a sesame paste, usually found in the international section of your grocery store. If unavailable, try peanut butter.

Combination of chickpeas and tofu produce a rich texture to these unusual burgers.

MAKE AHEAD

Prepare patties and sauce up to 1 day advance. Bake just before serving.

PER SERVING (5)

Calories	226
Protein	15 g
Fat, total	10 g
Fat, saturated	2 g
Carbohydrates	21 g
Sodium	280 mg
Cholesterol	44 mg
Fiber	3 g

Vegetarian Shepherd's Pie with Peppered Potato Topping

◆■◆■□◆◆■◆□◆◆■◆

SERVES 6 TO 8

TIP

This shepherd's pie rivals the beef version — creamy, thick and rich tasting. Beans provide the meat-like texture.

For a different twist, try sweet potatoes.

Try other cheeses such as mozzarella or Swiss.

MAKE AHEAD

Prepare up to 1 day in advance. Reheat gently.

Freeze for up to 3 weeks.

Preheat oven to 350° F (180° C)

13- by 9-inch (3 L) baking dish

2 tsp	vegetable oil	10 mL
2 tsp	minced garlic	10 mL
1 cup	chopped onions	250 mL
3/4 cup	finely chopped carrots	175 mL
1 1/2 cups	prepared tomato pasta sauce	375 mL
1 cup	canned red kidney beans, rinsed and drained	250 mL
1 cup	canned chickpeas, rinsed and drained	250 mL
1/2 cup	BASIC VEGETABLE STOCK (see recipe, page 36) *or* water	125 mL
1 1/2 tsp	dried basil	7 mL
2	bay leaves	2
4 cups	diced potatoes	1 L
1/2 cup	2% milk	125 mL
1/3 cup	light sour cream	75 mL
1/4 tsp	freshly ground black pepper	1 mL
3/4 cup	shredded Cheddar cheese	175 mL
3 tbsp	grated Parmesan cheese	45 mL

1. In a saucepan heat oil over medium-high heat. Add garlic, onions and carrots; cook 4 minutes or until onion is softened. Stir in tomato sauce, kidney beans, chickpeas, stock, basil and bay leaves; reduce heat to medium-low, cover and cook 15 minutes or until vegetables are tender. Remove bay leaves. Transfer sauce to a food processor; pulse on and off just until chunky. Spread over bottom of baking dish.

2. Place potatoes in a saucepan; add cold water to cover. Bring to a boil, reduce heat and simmer 10 to 12 minutes or until tender. Drain; mash with milk, sour cream and pepper. Spoon on top of sauce in baking dish. Sprinkle with cheeses.

3. Bake, uncovered, 20 minutes or until hot.

PER SERVING (8)	
Calories	238
Protein	11 g
Fat, total	7 g
Fat, saturated	2.0 g
Carbohydrates	36 g
Sodium	522 mg
Cholesterol	10 mg
Fiber	5 g

Vegetable and Goat Cheese Pie in Olive Oil Crust

◆■◆■◆■◆◀━━▶■◆■◆■◆

Preheat oven to 400° F (200° C)

9-inch (2.5 L) springform pan *or* 9-inch (23 cm) deep-dish pie plate

SERVES 6

TIP

This wonderful crust was inspired by fellow Robert Rose author Byron Ayanoglu in his book, *The New Vegetarian Gourmet*. Olive oil provides a rich, creamy texture without butter. Do not overbake.

Substitute other vegetables if desired.

Italian seasoning can be replaced with dried basil.

MAKE AHEAD

Make crust up to 1 day in advance.

If dicing potatoes ahead of time, cover with cold water to prevent browning.

Prepare filling early in day; bake before serving.

PER SERVING

Calories	275
Protein	8 g
Fat, total	11 g
Fat, saturated	2.0 g
Carbohydrates	37 g
Sodium	273 mg
Cholesterol	37 mg
Fiber	3 g

Crust

1 1/4 cups	all-purpose flour	300 mL
2 tbsp	grated Parmesan cheese	15 mL
1 tsp	baking powder	5 mL
1 tsp	dried basil	5 mL
1/4 tsp	freshly ground black pepper	1 mL
1	egg	1
1/4 cup	2% milk	50 mL
3 tbsp	olive oil	45 mL

Filling

1 1/2 cups	diced potatoes	375 mL
2 tsp	vegetable oil	10 mL
2 tsp	minced garlic	10 mL
1 cup	chopped leeks	250 mL
1/2 cup	chopped red bell peppers	125 mL
1 1/2 cups	sliced mushrooms	375 mL
1 1/2 cups	chopped zucchini	375 mL
1 tsp	Italian seasoning	5 mL
3/4 cup	prepared tomato pasta sauce	175 mL
1 1/2 oz	goat cheese	40 g

1. Make the crust: In a food processor, combine flour, Parmesan, baking powder, basil and pepper. In a small bowl, whisk together egg, milk and olive oil. With machine running, add liquid ingredients through the feed tube; pulse on and off until mixed and crumbly. Pat onto bottom and sides of springform pan or pie plate. (Pastry will only reach part way up sides of springform pan; turn edge under to even.) Bake 15 minutes or until lightly browned.

2. Meanwhile, make the filling: In a small saucepan, add cold water to cover to potatoes. Bring to a boil; cook 10 minutes or until tender when pierced with tip of a knife. Drain; set aside. In a nonstick saucepan sprayed with vegetable spray, heat oil over medium heat. Cook garlic, leeks and red peppers 4 minutes. Stir in mushrooms, zucchini and Italian seasoning; cook 6 minutes or until tender. Stir in pasta sauce and cooked potatoes; pour into baked crust. Dot with goat cheese.

3. Bake 10 minutes, or until heated through and goat cheese has melted.

Bean and Sweet Potato Chili on Garlic Polenta

TIP

Use any cooked beans that you have on hand.

Try fresh fennel instead of leeks.

Polenta is delicious, nutritious and takes minutes to make.

A great source of fiber.

MAKE AHEAD

Prepare chili up to 2 days in advance. Cook polenta just before serving.

PER SERVING

Calories	327
Protein	11 g
Fat, total	3 g
Fat, saturated	0.3 g
Carbohydrates	65 g
Sodium	362 mg
Cholesterol	0 mg
Fiber	10 g

Chili

2 tsp	vegetable oil	10 mL
1 1/2 tsp	minced garlic	7 mL
1 1/2 cups	chopped leeks	375 mL
1 cup	chopped red bell peppers	250 mL
1	can (19 oz [540 mL]) tomatoes, puréed	1
1 1/2 cups	canned red kidney beans, rinsed and drained	375 mL
1 1/4 cups	chopped peeled sweet potatoes	300 mL
1 tbsp	fennel seeds	15 mL
2 tsp	chili powder	10 mL
1 tsp	dried basil	5 mL

Polenta

3 1/4 cups	BASIC VEGETABLE STOCK (see recipe, page 36)	800 mL
1 cup	cornmeal	250 mL
1 tsp	minced garlic	5 mL

1. In a large nonstick saucepan, heat oil over medium-high heat. Add garlic, leeks and red peppers; cook 4 minutes or until softened. Stir in tomatoes, beans, sweet potatoes, fennel seeds, chili powder and basil; bring to a boil. Reduce heat to medium-low, cover and cook 20 to 25 minutes or until sweet potatoes are tender.

2. Meanwhile, in a deep saucepan, bring vegetable stock to a boil. Reduce heat to low and gradually whisk in cornmeal and garlic. Cook 5 minutes, stirring frequently.

3. Pour polenta into a serving dish. Spoon chili over top. Serve immediately.

Zucchini, Mushroom and Bean Loaf with Tomato Sauce

◆■◆■□◆◀▬▬▶◆□■◆■◆

SERVES 6 TO 8

TIP

This is my favorite vegetarian loaf, which tastes a lot like chicken. The combination of puréed beans provides a meaty texture.

Replace bottled chili sauce with barbecue sauce or ketchup.

This loaf is a good source of fiber.

MAKE AHEAD

Prepare up to 1 day in advance and serve cold or reheated.

PER SERVING (8)	
Calories	190
Protein	11 g
Fat, total	4 g
Fat, saturated	1 g
Carbohydrates	30 g
Sodium	489 mg
Cholesterol	55 mg
Fiber	8 g

Preheat oven to 350° F (180° C)

9- by 5-inch (2 L) loaf pan sprayed with vegetable spray

1 tsp	vegetable oil	5 mL
2 tsp	minced garlic	10 mL
1 cup	chopped onions	250 mL
1/2 cup	finely chopped carrots	125 mL
2 cups	chopped zucchini	500 mL
1 cup	chopped mushrooms	250 mL
1 1/2 cups	canned chickpeas, rinsed and drained	375 mL
1 1/2 cups	canned white kidney beans, rinsed and drained	375 mL
1/3 cup	dry seasoned bread crumbs	75 mL
3 tbsp	chili sauce	45 mL
2 tbsp	grated Parmesan cheese	25 mL
2	eggs	2
1 tsp	dried basil	5 mL
3/4 cup	prepared tomato pasta sauce	175 mL

1. In a nonstick frying pan, heat oil over medium-high heat. Add garlic, onions and carrots; cook 4 minutes. Stir in zucchini and mushrooms; cook 8 minutes or until softened.

2. In a food processor, combine zucchini mixture, chickpeas, white kidney beans, seasoned bread crumbs, chili sauce, Parmesan, eggs and basil. Pulse on and off until finely chopped and well combined. Press into prepared loaf pan.

3. Bake, uncovered, about 40 minutes or until tester inserted in center comes out clean. Heat tomato sauce and serve with sliced loaf.

Falafel with Tahini Lemon Dressing

TIP

Falafels are a wonderful delicacy from the Middle East. Traditionally, they are deep-fried, making them high in fat and calories. This baked version is better tasting and healthier.

Tahini lemon dressing can be replaced with any other low-fat dressing.

Tahini can be found in the international section of grocers. If unavailable, try smooth peanut butter.

MAKE AHEAD

Prepare falafels up to 1 day in advance. Best if baked just before serving.

Nutrition note: Values given below are for each of 6 servings, with each serving accompanied by 2 tsp (10 mL) dressing.

PER SERVING (6)

Calories	264
Protein	11 g
Fat, total	6 g
Fat, saturated	1 g
Carbohydrates	41 g
Sodium	415 mg
Cholesterol	36 mg
Fiber	5 g

Preheat oven to 400° F (200° C)
Baking sheet sprayed with vegetable spray

1	can (19 oz [540 mL]) chickpeas, rinsed and drained	540 mL
1/4 cup	chopped green onions	50 mL
1/4 cup	chopped fresh coriander	50 mL
1/4 cup	bread crumbs	50 mL
2 tbsp	tahini	25 mL
1 tbsp	freshly squeezed lemon juice	15 mL
1 1/2 tsp	minced garlic	7 mL
1/4 tsp	baking powder	1 mL
1/4 tsp	ground cumin	1 mL
1	egg	1
	Freshly ground black pepper, to taste	
4	small pita breads	4
Half	recipe CREAMY TAHINI LEMON DRESSING (see recipe, page 61)	Half

Garnish (optional)

Tomato slices
Lettuce leaves

1. In a food processor, combine chickpeas, green onions, coriander, bread crumbs, tahini, lemon juice, garlic, baking powder, cumin, egg and pepper. Pulse on and off until well-mixed. Form into 16 balls of 2 tbsp (25 mL) each; flatten slightly. Put on prepared baking sheet.

2. Bake chickpea balls 20 minutes, turning at halfway point, or until golden.

3. Serve in pita breads with CREAMY TAHINI LEMON DRESSING and, if desired, tomato slices and lettuce.

Butternut Squash with Maple Syrup

SERVES 6 TO 8

TIP

Substitute sweet potato for squash.

For a gingerbread taste, try adding 1 tbsp (15 mL) molasses and reducing maple syrup to 3 tbsp (45 mL).

Egg whites can now be purchased in containers at grocery stores.

MAKE AHEAD

Prepare recipe to end of Step 1 up to 2 days in advance.

Can be baked early in the day and reheated.

Preheat oven to 350° F (180° C)

8-inch (2 L) square baking dish sprayed with vegetable spray

1 lb	diced peeled butternut squash	500 g
1/3 cup	dried bread crumbs	75 mL
1/4 cup	light sour cream	50 mL
1/4 cup	maple syrup	50 mL
2 tsp	margarine *or* butter	10 mL
2 tsp	grated orange zest	10 mL
3/4 tsp	ground cinnamon	4 mL
1/4 tsp	ground ginger	1 mL
3	eggs, separated	3
1/2 cup	canned corn kernels, drained	125 mL
Pinch	salt	Pinch

1. In a pot of boiling water, cook squash 8 minutes or until tender; drain. Put in a food processor along with bread crumbs, sour cream, maple syrup, margarine, orange zest, cinnamon, ginger and 2 egg yolks. (Discard third egg yolk.) Process until smooth. Transfer to a large bowl; cool. Add corn.

2. In a bowl with an electric mixer, beat 3 egg whites with salt until stiff peaks form. Stir one-quarter of egg whites into squash mixture. Gently fold remaining egg whites into squash mixture. Pour into prepared pan. Bake 25 minutes or until set.

PER SERVING (8)

Calories	99
Protein	3 g
Fat, total	3 g
Fat, saturated	1.0 g
Carbohydrates	17 g
Sodium	122 mg
Cholesterol	57 mg
Fiber	0 g

Caramelized Balsamic Onions with Chopped Dates

TIP

Use this wonderful onion dish as a vegetable side dish or as a topping over cooked pasta or other grains.

On non-vegetarian days these onions make a great topping for chicken, fish or beef.

MAKE AHEAD

Prepare early in day and reheat before serving.

2 tsp	margarine *or* butter	10 mL
2 tsp	minced garlic	10 mL
1 1/2 lbs	onions, thinly sliced	750 g
1/2 cup	chopped dates	125 mL
3 tbsp	balsamic vinegar	45 mL
1 tbsp	brown sugar	15 mL

1. In a large nonstick saucepan, melt margarine over medium heat. Add garlic and onions; cook, stirring occasionally, until soft and brown, about 20 minutes.

2. Stir in dates, vinegar and brown sugar; cook 10 minutes, stirring occasionally.

PER SERVING	
Calories	153
Protein	3 g
Fat, total	2 g
Fat, saturated	0.3 g
Carbohydrates	34 g
Sodium	32 mg
Cholesterol	0 mg
Fiber	5 g

Sugar Snap Peas with Sesame Sauce

SERVES 4

TIP

Use snow peas or green beans instead of the sugar snap peas.

MAKE AHEAD

Prepare sauce up to 2 days in advance.

Best cooked right before serving.

1 tbsp	honey	15 mL
1 tbsp	rice wine vinegar	15 mL
1 tbsp	sesame oil	15 mL
1 tbsp	soya sauce	15 mL
1/2 tsp	minced garlic	2 mL
1 lb	sugar snap peas, trimmed	500 g
1 tsp	vegetable oil	5 mL
1 tbsp	toasted sesame seeds	15 mL

1. In a small bowl, combine honey, vinegar, sesame oil, soya sauce and garlic; set aside.

2. Steam or boil sugar peas 2 minutes. In a large non-stick skillet sprayed with vegetable spray, heat oil over medium-high heat; cook peas for 3 minutes or until tender-crisp. Pour sauce over peas; cook until heated through. Serve immediately, sprinkled with sesame seeds.

PER SERVING

Calories	116
Protein	3 g
Fat, total	6 g
Fat, saturated	1.0 g
Carbohydrates	15 g
Sodium	269 mg
Cholesterol	0 mg
Fiber	2 g

Spinach Roll with Cheese Dill Filling

TIP

If ricotta mixture seems dry, add an extra 1 or 2 tbsp (15 or 25 mL) 2% milk.

Roll may crack. Don't worry; just keep rolling.

Use 1 package (10 oz [300 g]) fresh spinach, if desired.

Roast your own red bell peppers or buy water-packed roasted red peppers.

MAKE AHEAD

Prepare filling up to 1 day in advance. Bake roll (to the end of Step 3) early in the day. Can be refrigerated for up to 2 days.

PER SERVING (8)	
Calories	126
Protein	11 g
Fat, total	4 g
Fat, saturated	3.0 g
Carbohydrates	9 g
Sodium	250 mg
Cholesterol	69 mg
Fiber	2 g

Preheat oven to 350° F (180° C)

10- by 15-inch (25 by 37.5 cm) jelly roll pan lined with parchment paper and sprayed with vegetable spray

Roll

1	package (10 oz [300 g]) frozen chopped spinach, thawed and squeezed dry	1
2	egg yolks	2
1/2 cup	light sour cream	125 mL
1/3 cup	chopped fresh dill	75 mL
1/3 cup	all-purpose flour	75 mL
4	egg whites	4
Pinch	salt	Pinch
1 tbsp	grated Parmesan cheese	15 mL

Filling

3/4 cup	5% ricotta cheese	175 mL
2 oz	softened light cream cheese	50 g
2 tbsp	grated Parmesan cheese	25 mL
3 tbsp	chopped green onions	45 mL
3 tbsp	chopped roasted red peppers	45 mL
2 tbsp	chopped fresh dill	25 mL
2 tbsp	2% milk	25 mL

1. In a food processor, purée spinach, egg yolks, sour cream, dill and flour until smooth. Transfer to a large bowl.

2. In a large bowl using an electric mixer, beat egg whites with salt until stiff peaks form. Stir one-quarter of egg whites into spinach mixture. Fold in remaining egg whites. Spoon onto prepared jelly roll pan and smooth top with spatula. Bake 10 to 12 minutes or until tester comes out clean. Let cool 5 minutes. Sprinkle with 1 tbsp (15 mL) Parmesan.

Roll carefully using a tea towel to assist. Keep towel inside the roll until it cools. Be sure to remove towel before filling!

3. Invert jelly roll pan onto a clean tea towel. Remove pan and gently remove parchment paper. Roll up spinach roll and tea towel along short end, keeping tea towel inside the roll. Allow to cool completely.

4. Make the filling: In a bowl using an electric mixer or whisk, beat together ricotta, cream cheese and 1 tbsp (15 mL) of the Parmesan until smooth. Stir in green onions, roasted red peppers, dill and milk. Unroll spinach roll. Sprinkle with remaining 1 tbsp (15 mL) Parmesan. Spread with ricotta filling. Tightly re-roll and place on serving dish.

5. Serve at room temperature. Cut into 1-inch (2.5 cm) slices with a serrated knife.

Caramelized Onion Phyllo Bake

TIP

This is an onion lover's dream. It tastes like a creamy onion quiche.

Phyllo pastry is much lower in fat and calories than regular pie pastry.

Replace dill and Swiss cheese with other variations of your choice.

When working with phyllo, work quickly and keep unused phyllo covered with a towel. Refreeze unused portion.

MAKE AHEAD

Cook onions early in the day. Assemble and bake just before serving. Phyllo is best when hot and crisp.

PER SERVING (8)

Calories	171
Protein	9 g
Fat, total	7 g
Fat, saturated	2.0 g
Carbohydrates	18 g
Sodium	179 mg
Cholesterol	63 mg
Fiber	1 g

Preheat oven to 375° F (190° C)
9-inch (2.5 L) springform pan

2 tsp	vegetable oil	10 mL
2 tsp	minced garlic	10 mL
1 1/2 lbs	sliced onions	750 g
2 tsp	packed brown sugar	10 mL
2	egg whites	2
2	eggs	2
1 cup	light sour cream	250 mL
1/2 cup	chopped fresh dill (or 2 tsp [10 mL] dried)	125 mL
1/2 cup	shredded Swiss cheese (about 2 oz [50 g])	125 mL
2 tbsp	grated Parmesan cheese	25 mL
1 tbsp	all-purpose flour	15 mL
6	sheets phyllo pastry	6
2 tsp	melted margarine or butter	10 mL
1 tbsp	grated Parmesan cheese	15 mL

1. In a large nonstick saucepan, heat oil over medium heat. Stir in garlic, onions, and sugar; cook 30 minutes, stirring occasionally, or until browned and very soft.

2. In a large bowl, whisk together egg whites, whole eggs, sour cream, dill, Swiss cheese, 2 tbsp (25 mL) Parmesan cheese and flour. Stir in cooked onions.

3. Arrange two sheets of phyllo on bottom and up the sides of springform pan. Brush with some melted margarine. Layer another two sheets of phyllo and brush with margarine; repeat. Pour in filling. Sprinkle with Parmesan. Fold phyllo sheet ends over top, enclosing filling completely. Brush with remaining margarine.

4. Bake 50 minutes. Let stand 10 minutes before cutting and serving.

Zucchini and Roasted Pepper Quiche

TIP

This tastes like a rich Quiche Lorraine — but without all the fat.

Roast your own red bell peppers or buy water-packed roasted red peppers.

If leeks are unavailable, substitute onions.

MAKE AHEAD

Prepare recipe to the end of Step 1 up to 2 days in advance.

Bake quiche early in day and reheat gently.

PER SERVING (6)	
Calories	166
Protein	9 g
Fat, total	7 g
Fat, saturated	3.0 g
Carbohydrates	18 g
Sodium	522 mg
Cholesterol	49 mg
Fiber	3 g

Preheat oven to 350° F (180° C)

8-inch (2 L) square baking dish spayed with vegetable spray

2 tsp	vegetable oil	10 mL
1 1/2 tsp	minced garlic	7 mL
1 1/2 cups	chopped leeks	375 mL
4 cups	diced zucchini	1 L
1 1/2 tsp	dried basil	7 mL
3/4 cup	diced roasted red peppers	175 mL
1/4 cup	all-purpose flour	50 mL
1/4 cup	cornmeal	50 mL
1 tsp	baking powder	5 mL
1/4 tsp	salt	1 mL
1/4 tsp	freshly ground black pepper	1 mL
1	egg	1
1	egg white	1
1/2 cup	shredded Cheddar cheese (about 2 oz [50 g])	125 mL
1/2 cup	2% milk	125 mL
1/2 cup	light sour cream	125 mL
3 tbsp	grated Parmesan cheese	45 mL

1. In a nonstick saucepan sprayed with vegetable spray, heat oil over medium heat. Add garlic and leeks; cook 4 minutes. Stir in zucchini and basil; cook 5 minutes longer or until vegetables are tender. Stir in roasted peppers; remove from heat and let cool.

2. In a large bowl, stir together flour, cornmeal, baking powder, salt and pepper. In a separate bowl, whisk together whole egg, egg white, Cheddar, milk, sour cream and 2 tbsp (25 mL) of the Parmesan. Add wet ingredients and cooled vegetables to dry ingredients; stir to combine. Spoon into prepared baking dish. Sprinkle with remaining Parmesan.

3. Bake 30 to 35 minutes or until cake tester inserted at center comes out clean.

Three-Mushroom Tomato Potato Stew

TIP

If using whole dried mushrooms, slice after soaking.

Use any combination of wild mushrooms. If not available, use common mushrooms.

Serve over pasta, rice, couscous or any other type of cooked grain.

If dried mushrooms are unavailable, substitute 2 cups (500 mL) sliced button mushrooms and add 1 cup (250 mL) more stock.

MAKE AHEAD

Prepare up to 1 day in advance. Reheat gently, adding more stock if too thick.

PER SERVING	
Calories	187
Protein	7 g
Fat, total	4 g
Fat, saturated	0.4 g
Carbohydrates	37 g
Sodium	254 mg
Cholesterol	0 mg
Fiber	7 g

1 cup	sliced dried mushrooms	250 mL
2 tsp	vegetable oil	10 mL
1 1/2 cups	chopped onions	375 mL
2 tsp	minced garlic	10 mL
1 cup	chopped carrots	250 mL
4 cups	thinly sliced oyster mushrooms	1 L
3 cups	thinly sliced button mushrooms	750 mL
2 cups	BASIC VEGETABLE STOCK (see recipe, page 36)	500 mL
1	can (19 oz [540 mL]) tomatoes	1
3/4 cup	chopped peeled sweet potatoes	175 mL
3/4 cup	chopped peeled potatoes	175 mL
2 tbsp	tomato paste	25 mL
2	bay leaves	2
1 tsp	dried basil	5 mL
1 tsp	dried thyme	5 mL
1/4 tsp	coarsely ground black pepper	1 mL

1. In a small bowl, add 2 cups (500 mL) boiling water to cover dried mushrooms. Soak 15 minutes. Drain, reserving soaking liquid; measure out 1 cup (250 mL).

2. In a large nonstick saucepan sprayed with vegetable spray, heat oil over medium-high heat. Add onions, garlic and carrots; cook, stirring occasionally, 5 minutes or until softened and browned. Stir in fresh mushrooms; cook 8 minutes longer, stirring occasionally, or until all liquid is absorbed.

3. Stir in dried mushrooms, reserved 1 cup (250 mL) mushroom liquid, stock, tomatoes, sweet potatoes, potatoes, tomato paste, bay leaves, basil, thyme and pepper. Bring to a boil, reduce heat to medium-low, cover, and cook 20 minutes or until potatoes are tender.

Cauliflower, Leek and Sweet Potato Strudel

SERVES 6 TO 8

TIP

Cauliflower and sweet potatoes are a great combination. Substitute broccoli and white potato for a change.

Phyllo pastry is a delicious low-fat alternative to other pastries and it's simple to use. Look for it in the freezer section of your grocery store. Work quickly and cover phyllo sheets with a towel until ready to use. Refreeze any remainders.

MAKE AHEAD

Prepare filling (to the end of Step 2) up to 1 day ahead. Fill a few hours before serving, cover and refrigerate. Bake just before serving.

PER SERVING (8)

Calories	188
Protein	6 g
Fat, total	6 g
Fat, saturated	3.0 g
Carbohydrates	27 g
Sodium	166 mg
Cholesterol	37 mg
Fiber	3 g

Preheat oven to 375° F (190° C)
Baking sheet sprayed with vegetable spray

2 tsp	vegetable oil	10 mL
2 tsp	minced garlic	10 mL
2 1/2 cups	chopped leeks	625 mL
2 cups	finely chopped cauliflower	500 mL
2 cups	finely chopped peeled sweet potatoes	500 mL
1 cup	BASIC VEGETABLE STOCK (see recipe, page 36)	250 mL
3 tbsp	cornmeal	45 mL
2 tsp	dried basil	10 mL
1/4 tsp	freshly ground black pepper	1 mL
1	egg	1
1/2 cup	shredded sharp Cheddar cheese (about 2 oz [50 g])	125 mL
2 tbsp	grated Parmesan cheese	25 mL
6	sheets phyllo pastry	6
2 tsp	melted margarine or butter	10 mL

1. In a large nonstick saucepan sprayed with vegetable spray, heat oil over medium heat. Cook garlic, leeks, cauliflower and sweet potatoes for 8 minutes, stirring often. Add stock, cornmeal, basil and pepper; reduce heat to low, cover and cook 15 minutes, stirring occasionally, or until vegetables are tender. Let cool.

2. Stir egg, Cheddar and Parmesan into cooled vegetable mixture.

3. Layer 2 phyllo sheets on work surface and brush sparingly with melted margarine. Top with 2 more phyllo sheets and brush with margarine. Lay last 2 phyllo sheets on top. Spread vegetable mixture over surface leaving a 1-inch (2.5 cm) border on all sides. Starting at long end, roll up tightly. Tuck ends under.

4. Transfer to prepared baking sheet. Brush with remaining melted margarine. Bake 25 minutes or until golden brown.

Carrot Roll with Artichoke Garlic Filling

◆■◆■◆■ ◆ ■◆■◆■◆

Preheat oven to 350° F (180° C)
15- by 10-inch (37.5 by 25 cm) jelly roll pan lined with parchment paper and sprayed with vegetable spray

Roll

2 cups	diced carrots	500 mL
2	egg yolks	2
1/3 cup	chopped fresh dill (or 2 tsp [10 mL] dried)	75 mL
1/3 cup	all-purpose flour	75 mL
3 tbsp	light sour cream	45 mL
1 1/2 tbsp	packed brown sugar	22 mL
4	egg whites	4
Pinch	salt	Pinch
2 tsp	dry bread crumbs	10 mL

Filling

Half	can (14 oz [398 mL]) artichoke hearts, drained	Half
1/2 cup	5% smooth ricotta cheese	125 mL
3 tbsp	light sour cream	45 mL
3 tbsp	chopped green onions	45 mL
1 1/2 tbsp	grated Parmesan cheese	20 mL
1/2 tsp	minced garlic	2 mL

1. Boil or steam carrots until tender; rinse under cold water and drain. Add carrots, yolks, dill, flour, sour cream and brown sugar to food processor; purée. Transfer to a large bowl.

2. In a separate bowl using an electric mixer, beat egg whites with salt until stiff peaks form. Stir one-quarter of egg whites into carrot mixture. Fold in remaining egg whites. Spoon onto prepared jelly roll pan and smooth top with spatula. Bake 10 to 12 minutes. Let cool 5 minutes. Sprinkle evenly with 1 tsp (5 mL) of the bread crumbs.

Roll carefully using a tea towel to assist. Keep towel inside the roll until it cools. Be sure to remove towel before filling!

3. Invert jelly roll pan onto a clean tea towel. Remove pan and gently remove parchment paper. Sprinkle with remaining 1 tsp (5 mL) bread crumbs. Roll up carrot roll along short end in tea towel. Allow to cool completely.

4. Meanwhile, make the filling: In a food processor, purée artichoke hearts, ricotta, sour cream, green onions, Parmesan and garlic until smooth.

5. Unroll carrot roll. Spread with artichoke filling and tightly re-roll.

6. Serve at room temperature. Cut into 1-inch (2.5 cm) slices with a serrated knife.

Mushroom Cheese Quesadillas with Avocado Dip

TIP

Instead of the large (10-inch [25 cm]) tortillas, you can use 6 of the small (6-inch [15 cm]) variety.

Avocado is high in calories and fat but using only one half in the dip cuts the calories considerably. Use the other half in salads.

The quesadillas are great even without the dip.

MAKE AHEAD

Prepare mushroom filling up to 1 day in advance.

Bake just before serving. If preparing dip earlier, squeeze some lemon juice over top to prevent browning.

PER SERVING	
Calories	337
Protein	13 g
Fat, total	16 g
Fat, saturated	6 g
Carbohydrates	36 g
Sodium	492 mg
Cholesterol	17 mg
Fiber	5 g

Preheat oven to 400° F (200° C)
Baking sheet sprayed with vegetable spray

2 tsp	vegetable oil	10 mL
2 tsp	minced garlic	10 mL
1 cup	chopped onions	250 mL
3/4 tsp	chili powder	4 mL
14 oz	mushrooms (preferably wild), sliced	425 g
1/3 cup	chopped black olives	75 mL
1/2 cup	shredded Swiss cheese	125 mL
3 tbsp	grated Parmesan cheese	45 mL
4	large (10-inch [25 cm]) flour tortillas	4

Avocado Dip

Half	ripe avocado, peeled	Half
1/2 cup	chopped tomatoes	125 mL
1/4 cup	finely diced red bell peppers	50 mL
2 tbsp	chopped green onions	25 mL
1 tbsp	light mayonnaise	15 mL
1 tbsp	freshly squeezed lemon juice	15 mL
3/4 tsp	minced garlic	4 mL
Pinch	chili powder	Pinch

1. In a large saucepan, heat oil over medium-high heat. Add garlic, onions and chili powder; cook 4 minutes or until softened. Stir in mushrooms; cook, stirring often, 8 minutes or until browned and liquid is absorbed. Remove from heat. Stir in olives. In a small bowl, combine Swiss cheese and Parmesan.

2. Lay 2 tortillas on baking sheet. Divide mushroom mixture between them and spread to within 1/2 inch (1 cm) of edges. Sprinkle with cheese mixture. Lay remaining two tortillas on top and press lightly.

3. Bake 10 minutes or until hot.

4. Meanwhile, prepare dip: In a bowl, combine avocado, tomatoes, red peppers, green onions, mayonnaise, lemon juice, garlic and chili powder; with a fork, mash until chunky. Serve on top of quesadillas.

Black Bean, Corn and Leek Frittata

TIP

Here's a great variation on the traditional omelet — but with less fat and cholesterol.

Replace beans and vegetables with other varieties of your choice.

Coriander can be replaced with dill, parsley and basil.

MAKE AHEAD

Combine entire mixture early in the day. Cook just before serving.

1 1/2 tsp	vegetable oil	7 mL
2 tsp	minced garlic	10 mL
3/4 cup	chopped leeks	175 mL
1/2 cup	chopped red bell peppers	125 mL
1/2 cup	canned or frozen corn kernels, drained	125 mL
1/2 cup	canned black beans, rinsed and drained	125 mL
1/3 cup	chopped fresh coriander	75 mL
2	eggs	2
3	egg whites	3
1/3 cup	2% milk	75 mL
1/4 tsp	salt	1 mL
1/4 tsp	freshly ground black pepper	1 mL
2 tbsp	grated Parmesan cheese	25 mL

1. In a nonstick saucepan sprayed with vegetable spray, heat oil over medium-high heat. Add garlic, leeks and red peppers; cook 4 minutes or until softened. Remove from heat; stir in corn, black beans and coriander.

2. In a bowl whisk together whole eggs, egg whites, milk, salt and pepper. Stir in cooled vegetable mixture.

3. Spray a 12-inch (30 cm) nonstick frying pan with vegetable spray. Heat over medium-low heat. Pour in frittata mixture. Cook 5 minutes, gently lifting sides of frittata to let uncooked egg mixture flow under frittata. Sprinkle with Parmesan. Cover and cook another 3 minutes or until frittata is set. Slip frittata onto serving platter.

4. Cut into wedges and serve immediately.

PER SERVING (6)	
Calories	101
Protein	7 g
Fat, total	4 g
Fat, saturated	1.1 g
Carbohydrates	10 g
Sodium	253 mg
Cholesterol	74 mg
Fiber	2 g

Black Bean Quesadillas with Spinach Cheese Filling

TIP

Feel free to replace beans, goat cheese and coriander with other choices you prefer.

When using frozen spinach, use a sharp knife to cut about one-half package (10 oz [300 g]); refreeze remaining portion.

MAKE AHEAD

Prepare entire mixture up to 1 day in advance. Bake just before serving.

Preheat oven to 425° F (220° C)
Two baking sheets sprayed with vegetable spray

2 tsp	vegetable oil	10 mL
2 tsp	minced garlic	10 mL
1 cup	chopped onions	250 mL
1/2 cup	well-squeezed, thawed frozen chopped spinach	125 mL
1 cup	canned black beans, rinsed and drained	250 mL
2 oz	goat cheese	50 g
1/3 cup	chopped fresh coriander	75 mL
1/3 cup	shredded part-skim mozzarella cheese (about 1 oz [25 g])	75 mL
1/3 cup	5% ricotta cheese	75 mL
6	small (6-inch [15 cm]) flour tortillas	6
1/3 cup	salsa	75 mL

1. In a nonstick frying pan, heat oil over medium-high heat. Add garlic and onions; cook 6 minutes or until softened. Stir in spinach and remove from heat. Mash 1/2 cup (125 mL) of the black beans. Add mashed beans and remaining whole beans to spinach mixture.

2. In a bowl combine goat cheese, coriander, mozzarella and ricotta.

3. Lay 3 tortillas on baking sheets. Divide bean mixture among tortillas and spread to within 1/2 inch (1 cm) of edges. Spread cheese mixture over beans and top with salsa. Top with 3 remaining tortillas and press gently to stick.

4. Bake 5 minutes or until heated through.

PER SERVING

Calories	393
Protein	20 g
Fat, total	13 g
Fat, saturated	4 g
Carbohydrates	49 g
Sodium	666 mg
Cholesterol	13 mg
Fiber	10 g

Portobello Mushroom Sandwiches with Spinach Cheese Dressing

SERVES 4

TIP

These mushroom sandwiches are almost beef-like in taste.

If pitas are not available, try whole-wheat hamburger buns.

Portobello mushrooms can be refrigerated in a paper bag for several days in the refrigerator.

If using whole portobello mushrooms, remove stems and save for soups or other dishes.

Use 1 1/2 cups (375 mL) fresh spinach to get 1/4 cup (50 mL) finely chopped cooked spinach.

Grill mushrooms if desired.

MAKE AHEAD

Prepare spinach dressing up to 2 days in advance.

Sauté mushrooms early in day. Reheat before serving.

PER SERVING

Calories	263
Protein	11 g
Fat, total	8 g
Fat, saturated	2.0 g
Carbohydrates	37 g
Sodium	328 mg
Cholesterol	10 mg
Fiber	1 g

1/4 cup	cooked spinach, well drained and finely chopped	50 mL
1/4 cup	5% ricotta cheese	50 mL
1/4 cup	shredded Swiss cheese (about 1 oz [25 g])	50 mL
2 tbsp	light mayonnaise	25 mL
1 tbsp	grated Parmesan cheese	15 mL
1 1/2 tsp	freshly squeezed lemon juice	7 mL
1 tsp	Dijon mustard	5 mL
1/2 tsp	minced garlic	2 mL
4	portobello mushroom caps (about 2 oz [50 g] each)	4
2 tsp	olive oil	10 mL
2	large pita breads, cut in half *or* 4 small pita breads, preferably whole wheat	2

Garnishes (optional)

Sliced tomatoes

Sliced onions

Lettuce leaves

1. In food processor or blender, purée spinach, ricotta, Swiss cheese, mayonnaise, Parmesan, lemon juice, mustard and garlic until smooth.

2. Wipe mushroom caps with a damp paper towel to clean. In a large nonstick frying pan sprayed with vegetable spray, heat oil over medium-high heat. Cook mushrooms 3 minutes per side or until tender when pierced with a fork and golden on both sides.

3. Put a hot mushroom cap into each pita and top with 2 tbsp (25 mL) spinach spread. If desired, garnish with tomatoes, onions and lettuce leaves. Serve hot.

Layered Tortilla Tomato and Cheese Pie

<table>
</table>

SERVES 8

TIP

Replace the beans with others of your choice.

For a sharper cheese flavor, try aged Cheddar or Swiss.

This is a visually attractive main meal — a vegetarian's delight.

MAKE AHEAD

Prepare filling up to 1 day in advance and layer early in day. Bake before serving.

Great to reheat.

PER SERVING

Calories	310
Protein	16 g
Fat, total	10 g
Fat, saturated	4.0 g
Carbohydrates	41 g
Sodium	746 mg
Cholesterol	18 mg
Fiber	7 g

Preheat oven to 350° F (180° C)
9-inch (2.5 L) springform pan sprayed with vegetable spray

2 tsp	vegetable oil	10 mL
2 tsp	minced garlic	10 mL
1/2 cup	chopped red onions	125 mL
1 cup	chopped red bell peppers	250 mL
1/2 cup	chopped green peppers	125 mL
1 1/2 cups	prepared tomato pasta sauce	375 mL
1 cup	canned corn kernels, drained	250 mL
1 tsp	dried basil	5 mL
1 tsp	chili powder	5 mL
1/2 tsp	ground cumin	2 mL
1 1/2 cups	canned black beans, rinsed and drained	375 mL
1 1/2 cups	canned white kidney beans, rinsed and drained	375 mL
1 cup	shredded part-skim mozzarella cheese (about 4 oz [125 g])	250 mL
1/2 cup	shredded Cheddar cheese (about 2 oz [50 g])	125 mL
2 tbsp	grated Parmesan cheese	25 mL
4	large (10-inch [25 cm]) flour tortillas	4

1. In a nonstick saucepan sprayed with vegetable spray, heat oil over medium heat. Add garlic and onions; cook 4 minutes, stirring occasionally. Stir in peppers; cook 3 minutes, stirring occasionally. Stir in tomato sauce, corn, basil, chili powder and cumin; cover and cook 4 minutes, stirring occasionally. Remove from heat.

2. In a bowl combine black beans and white kidney beans. Mash roughly and stir into vegetable mixture.

3. In a small bowl, combine mozzarella, Cheddar and Parmesan cheeses.

4. Place a tortilla in prepared springform pan. Spread with one-third of the vegetable-bean sauce. Sprinkle with one-third of the cheese mixture. Repeat layers twice; top with final tortilla. Cover pan tightly with foil.

5. Bake 20 minutes or until heated through and cheese has melted. Cut into wedges with a sharp knife.

Potato Crust Pesto Pizza

TIP

Using potatoes for a pizza crust instead of bread is unusual and delicious.

Homemade pesto can be replaced with the store-bought variety, although it may contain more fat and calories.

Vary this recipe with different toppings of your choice.

MAKE AHEAD

Prepare pizza up to 1 day in advance. Bake just before serving.

Great for leftovers.

Preheat oven to 425° F (220° C)
10-inch (3 L) springform pan sprayed with vegetable spray

3 cups	diced potatoes	750 mL
2 tbsp	olive oil	25 mL
1 cup	all-purpose flour	250 mL
2 tbsp	grated Parmesan cheese	25 mL
1 tsp	dried basil	5 mL
1/4 tsp	salt	1 mL
1/4 tsp	freshly ground black pepper	1 mL
1/3 cup	CREAMY PESTO SAUCE (see recipe, page 68)	75 mL
1/4 cup	sliced black olives	50 mL
1/4 cup	thinly sliced red bell peppers	50 mL
1/2 cup	shredded part-skim mozzarella cheese (about 2 oz [50 g])	125 mL

1. In a saucepan add cold water to cover potatoes. Bring to a boil; cook 10 minutes or until tender when pierced with the tip of a knife. Drain; mash with oil. Stir in flour, Parmesan, basil, salt and pepper until well mixed. Do not overmix. Press onto bottom of prepared pan. Bake 15 minutes or until golden at edges.

2. Spread with pesto. Sprinkle with black olives, red peppers and mozzarella. Return to oven; bake 10 minutes.

PER SERVING

Calories	299
Protein	9 g
Fat, total	10 g
Fat, saturated	3.0 g
Carbohydrates	44 g
Sodium	217 mg
Cholesterol	7 mg
Fiber	4 g

PASTA AND GRAINS

Curried Squash Risotto with Apricots and Dates

TIP

True risotto requires that you add hot liquid in small amounts, stirring constantly until absorbed. Use this technique (if you have time) for a creamier texture. (Keep in mind that you'll also need to add a larger quantity of stock.)

Try replacing squash with diced sweet potatoes.

Try any dried fruit in place of apricots and dates.

Try brown rice instead of white; cook the rice separately in stock until tender, about 40 minutes.

MAKE AHEAD

Prepare up to 1 day in advance. Reheat gently.

1 tsp	vegetable oil	5 mL
2 tsp	minced garlic	10 mL
3/4 cup	chopped onions	175 mL
1 1/2 tsp	curry powder	7 mL
3/4 cup	wild rice	175 mL
3/4 cup	white rice	175 mL
3 1/2 cups	BASIC VEGETABLE STOCK (see recipe, page 36)	875 mL
1 cup	diced butternut squash	250 mL
1/3 cup	chopped dried apricots	75 mL
1/3 cup	chopped dates	75 mL

1. In a nonstick saucepan sprayed with vegetable spray, heat oil over medium heat. Add garlic, onions and curry powder; cook 4 minutes or until softened. Add wild rice and white rice; cook, stirring, 2 minutes.

2. Add the stock; bring to a boil. Reduce heat to low, cover and cook 20 minutes. Stir in squash. Increase heat to medium; cover and cook another 10 minutes or until liquid is absorbed and rice and squash are tender.

3. Stir in apricots and dates. Let stand, covered, 10 minutes before serving.

PER SERVING (6)

Calories	223
Protein	6 g
Fat, total	1 g
Fat, saturated	0.1 g
Carbohydrates	49 g
Sodium	10 mg
Cholesterol	0 mg
Fiber	3 g

POLENTA CUBES WITH GOAT CHEESE VEGETABLE SAUCE (PAGE 130) ➤
OVERLEAF: LINGUINE WITH CARAMELIZED ONIONS, TOMATOES AND BASIL (PAGE 147)

Barley Cabbage Rolls in Tomato Basil Sauce

◆■■◆■◆■■◆━━◆━━■◆■■◆◆■◆◆◆•

MAKES 8 TO 10

TIP

Here's a fabulous variation of traditional cabbage rolls. The nutritious barley is well suited to a vegetarian diet.

Barley is available in "pearl" and "pot" varieties; whichever you use, cook until tender.

If you like extra sauce, double the tomato sauce recipe.

MAKE AHEAD

Prepare filled rolls up to 2 days in advance.

Can be reheated.

Freeze up to 3 weeks

PER ROLL (10)	
Calories	88
Protein	3 g
Fat, total	2 g
Fat, saturated	0.2 g
Carbohydrates	17 g
Sodium	185 mg
Cholesterol	0 mg
Fiber	4 g

2 1/2 cups	BASIC VEGETABLE STOCK (see recipe, page 36)	625 mL
1/2 cup	barley	125 mL
1	bay leaf	1
1 1/2 tsp	dried basil	7 mL
1	large green cabbage	1
1 tsp	vegetable oil	5 mL
2 tsp	minced garlic	10 mL
1/2 cup	chopped onions	125 mL
1/2 cup	chopped green peppers	125 mL
1 cup	chopped plum tomatoes	250 mL
1/4 cup	chopped black olives	50 mL
2 tsp	drained capers	10 mL
1	can (19 oz [540 mL]) tomatoes	1
1 tbsp	packed brown sugar	15 mL
1 tbsp	tomato paste	15 mL
1 tsp	dried basil	5 mL

1. In a saucepan bring stock to a boil. Stir in barley, bay leaf and basil; cover, reduce heat to medium-low and cook 40 minutes or until barley is tender. Remove bay leaf.

2. Meanwhile, remove as much of cabbage core as possible. In a large pot of boiling water, cook cabbage 20 to 25 minutes. Drain. When cool enough to handle, separate leaves carefully.

3. In a nonstick frying pan, heat oil over medium-high heat. Add garlic, onions and green peppers; cook 4 minutes or until softened. Stir in tomatoes, black olives and capers. Cook 2 minutes or until tomatoes start to break up. Stir into cooked barley.

4. Put approximately 1/3 cup (75 mL) barley filling in center of cabbage leaf; fold in sides and roll up. Repeat with remaining filling.

5. In a food processor, purée tomatoes, sugar, tomato paste and basil. Transfer to a large saucepan. Bring tomato sauce to a boil; reduce heat to low and place cabbage rolls into simmering sauce. Cover and cook 1 1/4 hours, turning rolls over at halfway point.

◄ RICE CAKES WITH TOMATO PURÉE (PAGE 142)

Polenta Cubes with Goat Cheese Vegetable Sauce

13- by 9-inch (3 L) baking dish sprayed with vegetable spray

TIP

Polenta is an excellent choice for a vegetarian main meal. It's delicious and nutritious.

To soften sun-dried tomatoes, pour boiling water over them and soak 15 minutes or until soft. Drain and chop.

MAKE AHEAD

Prepare to end of Step 3 earlier in day. Bring sauce back to a simmer before proceeding with Step 4.

Polenta Cubes

4 cups	BASIC VEGETABLE STOCK (see recipe, page 36)	1 L
2 cups	cornmeal	500 mL
1/8 tsp	cayenne pepper	0.5 mL
2 tbsp	grated Parmesan cheese	25 mL
1 1/2 tsp	minced garlic	7 mL

Sauce

2 tsp	vegetable oil	10 mL
2 tsp	minced garlic	10 mL
2 cups	chopped leeks	500 mL
2 cups	chopped red bell peppers	500 mL
1 1/2 cups	BASIC VEGETABLE STOCK (see recipe, page 36)	375 mL
2/3 cup	chopped softened sun-dried tomatoes (see Tip, at left)	150 mL
1/2 cup	sliced black olives	125 mL
2 tsp	dried basil	10 mL
4 oz	goat cheese, crumbled	125 g
2 tbsp	balsamic vinegar	25 mL

1. In a deep saucepan, bring vegetable stock to a boil. Reduce heat to low and gradually whisk in cornmeal and cayenne pepper. Cook 5 minutes, stirring frequently. Stir in Parmesan and garlic. Spoon into prepared baking dish, using the back of a wet spoon to smooth top. Cover and chill while making sauce.

2. In a large nonstick saucepan sprayed with vegetable spray, heat oil over medium-high heat. Add garlic, leeks and red peppers; cook 5 to 8 minutes until soft and slightly browned. Stir in vegetable stock, sun-dried tomatoes, olives and basil; reduce heat to medium, cover and cook 4 minutes.

PER SERVING (8)	
Calories	239
Protein	7 g
Fat, total	7 g
Fat, saturated	1.0 g
Carbohydrates	41 g
Sodium	278 mg
Cholesterol	1 mg
Fiber	6 g

3. Meanwhile, turn cooled polenta onto a cutting board. Cut into 1/2-inch (1 cm) squares.

4. Stir goat cheese and vinegar into sauce until cheese melts. Stir in polenta cubes; cook, stirring, 4 minutes or until heated through. Serve immediately.

Sun-Dried Tomato Mushroom Polenta Squares

SERVES 4 TO 6

TIP

To soften sun-dried tomatoes, pour boiling water over them and soak 15 minutes or until soft. Drain and chop.

Cornmeal is a nutritious, delicious grain for vegetarian diets. It's extremely versatile.

Great served as an entire meal or as an appetizer. Make sauce if serving as an appetizer.

MAKE AHEAD

Prepare squares up to 1 day in advance and coat with topping. Bake just before serving.

Preheat oven to 400° F (200° C)
8-inch (2 L) square baking dish sprayed with vegetable spray
Baking sheet sprayed with vegetable spray

1 tsp	vegetable oil	5 mL
2 tsp	minced garlic	10 mL
1/2 cup	chopped onions	125 mL
1 3/4 cups	chopped mushrooms	425 mL
1 1/2 tsp	dried basil	7 mL
1/2 cup	chopped softened sun-dried tomatoes (see Tip, at left)	125 mL
1 tbsp	grated Parmesan cheese	15 mL
2 1/2 cups	BASIC VEGETABLE STOCK (see recipe, page 36)	625 mL
1 cup	cornmeal	250 mL
1	egg white	1
3 tbsp	2% milk *or* water	45 mL
1/2 cup	seasoned dry bread crumbs	125 mL
2 tbsp	grated Parmesan cheese	25 mL

Sauce (optional)

1/3 cup	light sour cream	75 mL
2 tbsp	light mayonnaise	25 mL
2 tsp	freshly squeezed lemon juice	10 mL
1 tsp	dried basil	5 mL

1. In a nonstick frying pan sprayed with vegetable spray, heat oil over medium-high heat. Add garlic and onions; cook 3 minutes or until softened. Add mushrooms and basil; cook, stirring frequently, 5 minutes or until mushrooms are browned. Remove from heat; stir in sun-dried tomatoes and 1 tbsp (15 mL) Parmesan cheese. Set aside.

PER SERVING (6)	
Calories	164
Protein	6 g
Fat, total	3 g
Fat, saturated	1.0 g
Carbohydrates	29 g
Sodium	238 mg
Cholesterol	3 mg
Fiber	4 g

2. In a deep saucepan, bring vegetable stock to a boil. Reduce heat to low and gradually whisk in corn-meal. Cook 5 minutes, stirring frequently. Stir vegetable mixture into polenta. Spoon into prepared baking dish, using the back of a wet spoon to smooth top. Cover and chill 30 minutes.

3. Meanwhile, in a small bowl, whisk egg white with milk. On a plate, stir together bread crumbs and 2 tbsp (25 mL) Parmesan cheese.

4. Turn cooled polenta onto a cutting board. Cut into 12 squares. Dip each square in egg wash, then coat with crumb mixture and place on prepared baking sheet.

5. Bake 15 minutes, turning at halfway point, or until golden and heated through. Meanwhile, prepare sauce, if desired.

6. Make the sauce: In a small bowl, stir together sour cream, mayonnaise, lemon juice and basil. Serve over polenta squares.

Vegetable and Cheese Cannelloni with Tomato Sauce

◆■■◆■◆■◆■◆ ◆■◆■◆■◆■◆

SERVES 6

TIP

To make stuffing easier, cut along one side of each cannelloni shell with a pair of scissors — lay flat, stuff and roll up.

Substitute 18 jumbo pasta shells and stuff each with 4 tsp (20 mL) filling.

To soften sun-dried tomatoes, pour boiling water over them and soak 15 minutes or until soft. Drain and chop.

MAKE AHEAD

Prepare up to 1 day in advance. Bake just before serving. Great to reheat.

Preheat oven to 350° F (180° C)
13- by 9-inch (3 L) baking dish

12	cannelloni noodles	12
1/4 cup	finely chopped carrots	50 mL
2 tsp	vegetable oil	10 mL
1 tsp	minced garlic	5 mL
1/2 cup	chopped red bell peppers	125 mL
1/3 cup	chopped red onions	75 mL
1/2 cup	chopped mushrooms	125 mL
1/3 cup	chopped softened sun-dried tomatoes (see Tip, at left)	75 mL
1/2 tsp	dried basil	2 mL
1/4 tsp	dried oregano	1 mL
1/4 tsp	freshly ground black pepper	1 mL
3/4 cup	5% ricotta cheese	175 mL
1/4 cup	light cream cheese	50 mL
3 tbsp	grated Parmesan cheese	45 mL
1	egg	1
1 cup	prepared tomato pasta sauce	250 mL
1/3 cup	shredded part-skim mozzarella cheese (about 1 1/2 oz [35 g]), optional	75 mL

1. In a large pot of boiling water, cook cannelloni 12 minutes or until tender but firm. Rinse under cold water, drain and set aside.

2. In a small saucepan, add cold water to cover carrots; bring to a boil and cook 3 minutes or just until tender. Drain; set aside.

PER SERVING

Calories	377
Protein	15 g
Fat, total	8 g
Fat, saturated	3.0 g
Carbohydrates	63 g
Sodium	640 mg
Cholesterol	52 mg
Fiber	11 g

3. In a large nonstick saucepan sprayed with vegetable spray, heat oil over medium-low heat. Add garlic, red peppers and red onions; cook 4 minutes or until vegetables are softened. Stir in mushrooms, sun-dried tomatoes, basil, oregano and pepper; cook 3 minutes or until vegetables are tender. Stir in cooked carrots.

4. In a bowl stir together vegetable mixture, ricotta, cream cheese, Parmesan and egg until well mixed.

4. Spoon 1/2 cup (125 mL) of the tomato sauce over bottom of baking dish. Stuff each cannelloni shell with 2 tbsp (25 mL) filling and place in baking dish. Top cannelloni with remaining tomato sauce, and mozzarella, if using.

5. Cover dish tightly with foil. Bake 20 minutes or until hot.

Sun-Dried Tomato and Leek Pasta Bake

TIP

To soften sun-dried tomatoes, pour boiling water over them and soak 15 minutes or until soft. Drain and chop.

Any small, shaped pasta works well in this recipe. Try macaroni or orzo.

MAKE AHEAD

Prepare up to 1 day in advance. Reheat gently.

Preheat oven to 350° F (180° C)

9-inch (2.5 L) springform pan lined with foil and sprayed with vegetable spray

1 cup	small shell pasta	250 mL
2 tsp	vegetable oil	10 mL
2 tsp	minced garlic	10 mL
1 1/2 cups	chopped leeks	375 mL
1 1/2 cups	sliced mushrooms	375 mL
1 cup	chopped red bell peppers	250 mL
1/2 cup	chopped softened sun-dried tomatoes (see Tip, at left)	125 mL
1/3 cup	sliced black olives	75 mL
2	eggs	2
2	egg whites	2
1 cup	2% evaporated milk	250 mL
1/2 cup	shredded part-skim mozzarella cheese (about 2 oz [50 g])	125 mL
2 tsp	dried basil	10 mL
3 oz	feta cheese, crumbled	75 g
2 tbsp	grated Parmesan cheese	25 mL

1. In a pot of boiling water, cook pasta 5 minutes or until tender but firm. Rinse under cold water, drain and set aside.

2. In a nonstick frying pan, heat oil over medium heat. Add garlic and leeks; cook 4 minutes or until softened. Stir in mushrooms and red peppers; cook 6 minutes or until vegetables are tender and moisture is absorbed. Stir in sun-dried tomatoes and black olives; remove from heat.

3. In a large bowl, whisk together whole eggs, egg whites, evaporated milk, mozzarella and basil. Stir in pasta, cooled vegetable mixture and feta. Pour into prepared pan. Sprinkle with Parmesan cheese.

4. Bake 30 to 35 minutes or until set.

PER SERVING (8)	
Calories	170
Protein	9 g
Fat, total	7 g
Fat, saturated	3 g
Carbohydrates	18 g
Sodium	316 mg
Cholesterol	68 mg
Fiber	2 g

Mediterranean Kasha Casserole with Sun-Dried Tomatoes

SERVES 6 TO 8

TIP

Kasha is a nutritious and delicious grain, often served with bow-tie pasta. This is a wonderful variation. Use whole-grain kasha to prevent sticking.

To soften sun-dried tomatoes, pour boiling water over them and soak 15 minutes or until soft. Drain and chop.

Either leave the cheese out or substitute one of your choice.

MAKE AHEAD

Prepare up to 2 days in advance. Reheat gently.

PER SERVING (8)

Calories	143
Protein	5 g
Fat, total	3 g
Fat, saturated	0.4 g
Carbohydrates	28 g
Sodium	325 mg
Cholesterol	0 mg
Fiber	3 g

3 cups	BASIC VEGETABLE STOCK (see recipe, page 36)	750 mL
1 cup	whole-grain kasha	250 mL
2 tsp	vegetable oil	10 mL
2 tsp	minced garlic	10 mL
1 cup	chopped onions	250 mL
1 1/2 cups	diced unpeeled eggplant	375 mL
1 1/2 cups	diced unpeeled zucchini	375 mL
2 cups	chopped mushrooms	500 mL
1 cup	diced plum tomatoes	250 mL
1 cup	prepared tomato pasta sauce	250 mL
1 tsp	dried basil	5 mL
1/2 tsp	dried oregano	2 mL
1/2 cup	chopped softened sun-dried tomatoes (see Tip, at left)	125 mL
1/3 cup	sliced black olives	75 mL
2 oz	feta cheese, crumbled (optional)	50 g

1. In a saucepan bring vegetable stock and kasha to a boil; reduce heat to low, cover and cook until liquid is absorbed, about 10 to 12 minutes.

2. Meanwhile, in a large nonstick saucepan sprayed with vegetable spray, heat oil over medium-high heat. Add garlic and onions; cook 2 minutes. Stir in eggplant and zucchini; cook 5 minutes, stirring often. Stir in mushrooms, tomatoes, tomato sauce, basil and oregano; cook 4 minutes, stirring occasionally. Remove from heat; stir in sun-dried tomatoes and olives.

3. Combine kasha with vegetable mixture. Serve sprinkled with feta cheese, if desired.

Oriental Rice Pizza with Hoisin

◆■■■◆■□■◆◆◆◆◆◆◆■◆■◆■◆◆

Preheat oven to 400° F (200° C)

10-inch (3 L) springform pan sprayed with vegetable spray

SERVES 6 TO 8

TIP

Try a combination of wild and white rice. Cook for 30 minutes over low heat, or try healthy and delicious brown rice.

Substitute different vegetables such as canned Chinese mushrooms, bamboo shoots or water chestnuts.

MAKE AHEAD

Prepare crust and sauce early in the day. Sauté vegetables just before serving, while baking crust.

PER SERVING (8)	
Calories	172
Protein	6 g
Fat, total	4 g
Fat, saturated	1.0 g
Carbohydrates	29 g
Sodium	526 mg
Cholesterol	27 mg
Fiber	2 g

Crust

2 cups	BASIC VEGETABLE STOCK (see recipe, page 36)	500 mL
1 cup	white or brown rice	250 mL
1	egg	1
1	egg white	1
1/4 cup	2% milk	50 mL
2 tbsp	soya sauce	25 mL
1 tsp	sesame oil	5 mL

Sauce

2 tbsp	hoisin sauce	25 mL
2 tbsp	rice wine vinegar	25 mL
1 tbsp	sesame oil	15 mL
1 tbsp	water	15 mL
1 1/2 tsp	honey	7 mL
1 tsp	cornstarch	5 mL

Filling

1 tsp	vegetable oil	5 mL
2 tsp	minced garlic	10 mL
1 1/2 tsp	minced ginger root	7 mL
1 cup	chopped broccoli	250 mL
1 cup	chopped red bell peppers	250 mL
1 cup	chopped snow peas	250 mL
1 cup	chopped baby corn cobs	250 mL

1. Make the crust: In a saucepan bring stock to a boil; stir in rice. Cover, reduce heat to medium-low and cook 15 minutes or until rice is tender and liquid absorbed. (If using brown rice, cook at least 35 minutes, adding an extra 1 cup [250 mL] stock.) Take off heat; let stand, covered, 5 minutes. Let rice cool.

2. In a bowl stir together cooked rice, whole egg, egg white, milk, soya sauce and sesame oil until well mixed. Press rice mixture onto bottom of prepared pan. Bake 12 minutes. Meanwhile, make sauce and filling.

3. Make the sauce: In a small bowl, whisk together hoisin sauce, rice wine vinegar, sesame oil, water, honey and cornstarch; set aside.

4. Make the filling: In a nonstick frying pan sprayed with vegetable spray, heat oil over high heat. Add garlic and ginger; cook 1 minute, stirring. Stir in broccoli, red peppers and snow peas; cook, stirring, 4 minutes or until tender-crisp. Stir sauce again and add to pan along with corn; cook, stirring, 30 seconds or until slightly thickened. Pour onto hot rice crust. Serve immediately.

Penne with Creamy White Bean Sauce

TIP

Use any medium-sized pasta, such as rotini or medium shells.

Puréed kidney beans give this sauce a texture similar to canned tuna.

Add other vegetables to replace red peppers and peas. Snow peas, broccoli or sliced green beans are good choices.

MAKE AHEAD

Prepare sauce early in the day. Sauté vegetables and cook pasta just before serving.

12 oz	penne	375 g
1	can (19 oz [540 mL]) white kidney beans, rinsed and drained	1
1 cup	BASIC VEGETABLE STOCK (see recipe, page 36), heated	250 mL
2 tbsp	olive oil	25 mL
2 tbsp	light mayonnaise	25 mL
1 tbsp	freshly squeezed lemon juice	15 mL
1 tbsp	drained capers	15 mL
1 1/2 tsp	minced garlic	7 mL
1/3 cup	chopped fresh dill (or 1 tbsp [15 mL] dried)	75 mL
1/4 tsp	freshly ground black pepper	1 mL
2 tsp	vegetable oil	10 mL
1 cup	chopped onions	250 mL
1 cup	chopped red bell peppers	250 mL
1 cup	fresh or frozen peas	250 mL

1. In a large pot of boiling water, cook penne 8 to 10 minutes or until tender but firm. Meanwhile, prepare the sauce.

2. In a food processor, combine beans, stock, olive oil, mayonnaise, lemon juice, capers, garlic, dill and pepper; process until well mixed.

3. In a nonstick frying pan, heat oil over medium-high heat. Add onions and red peppers; cook 4 minutes or until browned. Stir in peas; cook 1 minute.

4. Toss drained pasta with bean mixture and vegetables. Serve immediately.

PER SERVING (6)	
Calories	400
Protein	15 g
Fat, total	8 g
Fat, saturated	1 g
Carbohydrates	69 g
Sodium	599 mg
Cholesterol	0 mg
Fiber	7 g

Orzo Spinach Mushroom Pie

TIP

Orzo is a small, rice-shaped pasta. Cook it as you would any pasta, in plenty of boiling water until tender but firm.

If orzo is unavailable, use small shell pasta or macaroni.

Substitute vegetables of your choice.

MAKE AHEAD

Can be prepared up to 1 day in advance. Reheat in oven

Great as leftovers.

Preheat oven to 350° F (180° C)
10-inch (3 L) springform pan sprayed with vegetable spray

Crust

1 cup	orzo	250 mL
1/3 cup	prepared tomato pasta sauce	75 mL
3 tbsp	grated Parmesan cheese	45 mL
1	egg	1

Topping

2 tsp	vegetable oil	10 mL
2 tsp	minced garlic	10 mL
1 cup	chopped onions	250 mL
2 cups	chopped mushrooms	500 mL
3/4 cup	frozen chopped spinach (about half 10-oz [300 g] package), thawed	175 mL
4 tsp	freshly squeezed lemon juice	20 mL
1 tsp	dried oregano	5 mL
1/8 tsp	freshly ground black pepper	0.5 mL
1 cup	5% ricotta cheese	250 mL
2 oz	feta cheese, crumbled	50 g
4 tsp	grated Parmesan cheese	20 mL

PER SERVING (8)

Calories	161
Protein	11 g
Fat, total	6 g
Fat, saturated	3.0 g
Carbohydrates	17 g
Sodium	253 mg
Cholesterol	44 mg
Fiber	2 g

1. In a pot of boiling water, cook orzo 8 to 10 minutes or until tender but firm. Rinse under cold water and drain. In a bowl combine orzo, pasta sauce, Parmesan and egg; press onto bottom of prepared pan. Bake 20 minutes.

2. Meanwhile, in a large nonstick frying pan, heat oil over high heat. Add garlic and onions; cook 4 minutes or until soft and browned. Stir in mushrooms; cook 5 minutes or until browned. Stir in spinach, lemon juice, oregano and pepper; cook 2 minutes. Remove from heat. Stir in ricotta and feta cheeses.

3. Spoon spinach-mushroom topping over baked crust. Sprinkle with Parmesan. Bake 15 minutes or until hot.

Rice Cakes with Tomato Purée

Preheat oven to 425° F (220° C)
Baking sheet sprayed with vegetable spray

TIPS

Serve these with soup and salad for an excellent complete meal. Or serve as a side dish.

These cakes can also be sautéed in a nonstick skillet sprayed with vegetable spray.

Try brown rice. Cook 35 minutes or until tender, adding more stock if necessary.

MAKE AHEAD

Prepare cakes up to 1 day in advance; keep refrigerated until ready to bake.

PER CAKE

Calories	114
Protein	6 g
Fat, total	3 g
Fat, saturated	1 g
Carbohydrates	16 g
Sodium	149 mg
Cholesterol	27 mg
Fiber	1 g

Rice Cakes

4 cups	BASIC VEGETABLE STOCK (see recipe, page 36)	1 L
1/2 cup	wild rice	125 mL
1/2 cup	white rice	125 mL
1 tsp	minced garlic	5 mL
1/2 cup	shredded part-skim mozzarella cheese (about 2 oz [50 g])	125 mL
1/4 cup	shredded Swiss cheese (about 1/2 oz [15 g])	50 mL
1/4 cup	chopped green onions	50 mL
2 tbsp	grated Parmesan cheese	25 mL
1 tsp	dried basil	5 mL
1	egg	1
2	egg whites	2

Sauce

1/2 cup	prepared tomato pasta sauce	125 mL
2 tbsp	2% milk	25 mL
1/4 tsp	dried basil	1 mL

1. In a saucepan bring stock to a boil; stir in wild rice and white rice; cover, reduce heat to medium-low and cook 35 minutes or until rice is tender. Let rice cool slightly. Drain any excess liquid. Rinse with cold water.

2. In a bowl stir together cooled rice, garlic, mozzarella, Swiss, green onions, Parmesan, basil, whole egg and egg whites until well mixed. Using a 1/4 cup (50 mL) measure, form mixture into 10 patties.

3. Place on prepared baking sheet. Bake approximately 10 minutes per side until browned.

4. Meanwhile, in a small saucepan, heat tomato sauce, milk and basil. Serve with rice cakes.

Artichoke Basil Pesto with Penne

12 oz	penne	375 g
1	can (14 oz [398 mL]) artichoke hearts, drained	1
1/2 cup	packed fresh basil leaves	125 mL
3 tbsp	grated Parmesan cheese	45 mL
3 tbsp	toasted pine nuts	45 mL
1 1/2 tsp	minced garlic	7 mL
3/4 cup	BASIC VEGETABLE STOCK (see recipe, page 36) *or* water	175 mL
3 tbsp	olive oil	45 mL

1. In a large pot of boiling water, cook penne 8 to 10 minutes or until tender but firm. Meanwhile, prepare the pesto.

2. In a food processor, combine artichoke hearts, basil, Parmesan, pine nuts and garlic; process until finely chopped. With motor running, add vegetable stock and oil through feed tube; process until smooth.

3. Toss drained pasta with pesto. Serve immediately.

SERVES 4 TO 6

TIP

If basil is not available, substitute parsley or spinach leaves.

Toast pine nuts in a non-stick skillet over high heat until browned.

After preparing sauce, if not using immediately, pour some lemon juice over top to prevent browning.

MAKE AHEAD

Best prepared just before serving. Artichoke mixture will darken with exposure to air. Sprinkle with lemon juice to prevent browning.

PER SERVING (6)

Calories	350
Protein	12 g
Fat, total	12 g
Fat, saturated	2 g
Carbohydrates	51 g
Sodium	167 mg
Cholesterol	3 mg
Fiber	4 g

Tortellini with Red Pepper Pesto

Preheat oven to broil

2	large red bell peppers	2
1/2 cup	packed fresh basil leaves	125 mL
3 tbsp	toasted pine nuts	45 mL
3 tbsp	grated Parmesan cheese	45 mL
1 to 1 1/2 tsp	minced garlic	5 to 7 mL
1/4 cup	BASIC VEGETABLE STOCK (see recipe, page 36) *or* water	50 mL
2 tbsp	olive oil	25 mL
1 lb	frozen cheese tortellini	500 g

1. Arrange oven rack 6 inches (15 cm) from broiler element. Broil peppers, turning often, 15 to 20 minutes or until charred. Cool. Remove and discard stem, skin and seeds; cut peppers into thin strips. Transfer to bowl of a food processor; process along with basil, pine nuts, Parmesan and garlic until finely chopped. With motor running, add stock and oil through feed tube; process until smooth.

2. In a large pot of boiling water, cook tortellini until tender but firm; drain. Toss with red pepper pesto. Serve immediately.

SERVES 4

TIP

After broiling peppers, place them in a paper bag and let rest 10 minutes. Skin can then be removed more easily.

Substitute 8 oz (250 g) water-packed roasted peppers, drained.

Toast pine nuts in a nonstick skillet over high heat for 2 to 3 minutes until browned.

MAKE AHEAD

Prepare sauce up to 2 days in advance or freeze for up to 4 weeks.

PER SERVING

Calories	463
Protein	18 g
Fat, total	18 g
Fat, saturated	3 g
Carbohydrates	61 g
Sodium	568 mg
Cholesterol	4 mg
Fiber	3 g

Curried Couscous with Tomatoes and Chickpeas

SERVES 4 TO 6

TIP

Great source of nutrition for vegetarians.

Coriander can be replaced with basil, dill or parsley.

Couscous is available in the rice section of grocery stores.

Try quinoa in this recipe.

MAKE AHEAD

Prepare up to 2 days in advance. Reheat gently.

2 cups	BASIC VEGETABLE STOCK (see recipe, page 36)	500 mL
1 1/2 cups	couscous	375 mL
1 tsp	vegetable oil	5 mL
3 cups	chopped plum tomatoes	750 mL
1/2 cup	BASIC VEGETABLE STOCK	125 mL
2 tsp	curry powder	10 mL
2 tsp	minced garlic	10 mL
2 cups	canned chickpeas, rinsed and drained	500 mL
3/4 cup	chopped fresh coriander	175 mL
1/2 cup	chopped green onions	125 mL

1. In a saucepan bring stock to a boil; stir in couscous, cover and remove from heat. Let stand 5 minutes; transfer to a serving bowl.

2. Meanwhile, in a large nonstick saucepan, heat oil over medium-high heat. Add tomatoes, stock, curry and garlic; cook, stirring, 5 minutes or until tomatoes begin to break up. Stir in chickpeas; cook 2 minutes or until heated through. Add to couscous along with coriander and green onions; toss to combine. Serve immediately.

PER SERVING (6)	
Calories	309
Protein	12 g
Fat, total	3 g
Fat, saturated	0.3 g
Carbohydrates	59 g
Sodium	154 mg
Cholesterol	0 mg
Fiber	6 g

Hoisin Stir-Fried Vegetables and Tofu over Rice Noodles

SERVES 4

TIP

Tofu is sold in the produce section of supermarkets. Be sure to use a firm or extra-firm variety or it will fall apart in the stir-fry.

Tofu can be replaced with 6 oz (175 g) cooked beans of your choice.

If rice noodles are unavailable, use regular pasta. Cook according to package directions.

MAKE AHEAD

Prepare sauce up to 2 days in advance. Stir-fry just before serving.

PER SERVING	
Calories	513
Protein	15 g
Fat, total	9 g
Fat, saturated	1 g
Carbohydrates	97 g
Sodium	1110 mg
Cholesterol	0 mg
Fiber	5 g

Sauce

1/3 cup	hoisin sauce	75 mL
1/3 cup	soya sauce	75 mL
1/4 cup	rice wine vinegar	50 mL
1/4 cup	packed brown sugar	50 mL
1 tsp	minced garlic	5 mL
1 tsp	minced ginger root	5 mL

Stir-Fry

8 oz	thin rice vermicelli	250 g
2 tsp	vegetable oil	10 mL
2 1/4 cups	chopped red bell peppers	550 mL
2 1/4 cups	chopped leeks	550 mL
2 cups	sliced mushrooms	500 mL
1 1/4 cups	shredded carrots	300 mL
1 1/4 cups	chopped zucchini	300 mL
6 oz	firm tofu, cubed	175 g

1. In a small bowl, whisk together hoisin, soya sauce, vinegar, brown sugar, garlic and ginger. Set aside.

2. Pour boiling water over noodles to cover; soak 10 minutes or until soft. Drain well.

3. In a nonstick wok or large saucepan sprayed with vegetable spray, heat oil over high heat. Add red peppers and leeks; stir-fry 4 minutes. Add mushrooms and stir-fry 2 minutes. Add carrots and zucchini; stir-fry 2 minutes or until vegetables are tender-crisp. Add noodles, tofu and sauce; stir-fry 2 minutes or until bubbly and hot. Serve immediately.

Linguine with Caramelized Onions, Tomatoes and Basil

SERVES 4

TIP

Try Vidalia onions when in season (usually in the spring).

If using fresh basil, you'll get a more pronounced flavor if you add the basil after the pasta is tossed with the sauce. (Dried basil is added during the cooking.)

MAKE AHEAD

Cook onions 1 day in advance. Reheat, then continue recipe.

2 tsp	vegetable oil	10 mL
2 tsp	minced garlic	10 mL
2 tbsp	packed brown sugar	25 mL
6 cups	thinly sliced red onions	1.5 L
2 cups	diced plum tomatoes	500 mL
3/4 cup	BASIC VEGETABLE STOCK (see recipe, page 36)	175 mL
1/2 cup	chopped fresh basil (or 1 1/2 tsp [7 mL] dried)	125 mL
1/4 tsp	freshly ground black pepper	1 mL
12 oz	linguine	375 g

1. In a large nonstick saucepan, heat oil over medium-low heat. Add garlic, sugar and red onions; cook, stirring often, 30 minutes or until browned and very soft.

2. Stir in tomatoes, stock, basil and pepper; cook 5 minutes longer or until heated through.

3. Meanwhile, in a pot of boiling water, cook linguine until tender but firm. Drain and toss with sauce.

PER SERVING	
Calories	508
Protein	16 g
Fat, total	5 g
Fat, saturated	0.4 g
Carbohydrates	102 g
Sodium	28 mg
Cholesterol	0 mg
Fiber	7 g

Two-Mushroom and Feta Cheese Lasagna

SERVES 6 TO 8

TIP

Any combination of mushrooms will do. Be exotic and try different kinds of wild mushrooms, such as portobello, chanterelles or cremini.

Great dish to reheat.

To soften sun-dried tomatoes, pour boiling water over them and soak 15 minutes or until soft. Drain and chop.

MAKE AHEAD

Prepare cheese mixture and sauce up to 2 days in advance.

Assemble entire lasagna 1 day in advance then bake.

Preheat oven to 350° F (180° C)

13- by 9-inch (3 L) baking dish

9	lasagna noodles	9

Cheese Mixture

2 cups	5% ricotta cheese	500 mL
1 cup	shredded part-skim mozzarella cheese (about 4 oz [125 g])	250 mL
1/2 cup	2% milk	125 mL
3 tbsp	grated Parmesan cheese	45 mL
1/2 tsp	freshly ground black pepper	2 mL

Sauce

2 tsp	vegetable oil	10 mL
2 tsp	minced garlic	10 mL
1 cup	chopped onions	250 mL
2 tsp	dried oregano	10 mL
4 cups	sliced mushrooms (about 12 oz [375 g])	1 L
4 cups	sliced oyster mushrooms (about 12 oz [375 g])	1 L
1/2 cup	sliced black olives	125 mL
1/2 cup	chopped softened sun-dried tomatoes (see Tip, at left)	125 mL
4 oz	feta cheese, crumbled	125 g
1 1/4 cups	BASIC VEGETABLE STOCK (see recipe, page 36), chilled	300 mL
1 cup	2% milk	250 mL
3 tbsp	all-purpose flour	45 mL
1 1/2 tsp	Dijon mustard	7 mL
2 tbsp	grated Parmesan cheese	25 mL

PER SERVING (8)	
Calories	381
Protein	25 g
Fat, total	14 g
Fat, saturated	8 g
Carbohydrates	40 g
Sodium	572 mg
Cholesterol	47 mg
Fiber	3 g

1. In a large pot of boiling water, cook lasagna 12 to 14 minutes or until tender but firm. Rinse under cold water, drain and set aside.

2. Prepare the cheese mixture: In a bowl stir together ricotta, mozzarella, milk, Parmesan and pepper; set aside.

3. Make the sauce: In a large nonstick frying pan sprayed with vegetable spray, heat oil over high heat. Add garlic, onions and oregano; cook 5 minutes or until browned. Stir in button mushrooms; cook, stirring frequently, 5 minutes or until mushrooms are browned. Stir in oyster mushrooms; cook, stirring frequently, 5 minutes or until mushrooms are browned and liquid is absorbed. Remove from heat. Stir in olives, sun-dried tomatoes and feta cheese; set aside.

4. In a saucepan whisk together vegetable stock, milk, flour and Dijon mustard until flour is dissolved. Cook over medium-high heat, whisking, 5 to 8 minutes or until thickened. Stir into mushroom mixture.

5. Arrange 3 noodles in bottom of baking dish. Top with one-third of mushroom sauce, then one-half of cheese mixture. Repeat layers. Layer remaining 3 noodles and remaining mushroom sauce; sprinkle with Parmesan cheese. Cover tightly with foil.

6. Bake 25 to 30 minutes or until hot.

Three-Cheese Creamy Pasta Bean Bake

TIP

Fettuccine, spaghetti or small shell pasta can replace linguine.

Try other bean combinations such as chick peas, navy beans or black beans.

Replace Italian seasoning with dried basil.

MAKE AHEAD

Prepare all elements of recipe, except for pasta, up to 2 days in advance.

Assemble early in the day, then bake.

Preheat oven to 350° F (180° C)
8-cup (2 L) casserole dish sprayed with vegetable spray

1 cup	shredded part-skim mozzarella cheese (about 4 oz [125 g])	250 mL
1 cup	5% ricotta cheese	250 mL
3/4 cup	light sour cream	175 mL
1/4 cup	2% milk	50 mL
2 tbsp	grated Parmesan cheese	25 mL
8 oz	linguine, broken into thirds	250 g
2 tsp	vegetable oil	10 mL
1 1/2 tsp	minced garlic	7 mL
1 cup	chopped onions	250 mL
1/2 cup	chopped green peppers	125 mL
2 cups	prepared tomato pasta sauce	500 mL
3/4 cup	canned red kidney beans, rinsed and drained	175 mL
3/4 cup	canned white kidney beans, rinsed and drained	175 mL
2 tsp	Italian seasoning	10 mL

Topping

1/3 cup	dry seasoned bread crumbs	75 mL
4 tsp	grated Parmesan cheese	20 mL
2 tsp	olive oil	10 mL

1. In a small bowl, stir together mozzarella, ricotta, sour cream, milk and Parmesan; set aside.

2. In a pot of boiling water, cook linguine 8 to 10 minutes or until tender but firm. Rinse under cold running water, drain and stir into cheese mixture.

PER SERVING	
Calories	404
Protein	22 g
Fat, total	9 g
Fat, saturated	4 g
Carbohydrates	59 g
Sodium	841 mg
Cholesterol	20 mg
Fiber	6 g

3. In a nonstick saucepan sprayed with vegetable spray, heat oil over medium-high heat. Add garlic, onions and green peppers; cook 3 minutes or until softened. Stir in tomato sauce, beans and Italian seasoning; reduce heat to low and cook 5 minutes.

4. Meanwhile, make the topping: In a small bowl, combine bread crumbs, Parmesan and olive oil; set aside.

5. Spoon one-half of pasta-cheese mixture into prepared casserole; top with half of bean mixture. Repeat layers. Sprinkle with bread crumb topping. Bake 25 minutes or until golden and hot.

Stir-Fried Vegetables in a Pasta Basket with Cashew Sauce

TIP

Try almonds, peanuts or another nut instead of cashews.

The decorative pasta basket can be difficult to slice. Instead of pouring stir-fry over basket, you can serve portions of the stir-fried vegetables, then break up basket and sprinkle on top.

MAKE AHEAD

Prepare basket and sauce up to 1 day in advance.

PER SERVING (6)	
Calories	285
Protein	9 g
Fat, total	7 g
Fat, saturated	1 g
Carbohydrates	48 g
Sodium	159 mg
Cholesterol	0 mg
Fiber	4 g

Preheat oven to 425° F (220° C)

9-inch (2.5 L) springform pan sprayed with vegetable spray

Pasta Basket

8 oz	vermicelli *or* spaghettini, broken into thirds	250 g
1 tbsp	sesame oil	15 mL

Sauce

1/4 cup	chopped cashews	50 mL
3 tbsp	water	45 mL
4 tsp	honey	20 mL
1 tbsp	freshly squeezed lemon juice	15 mL
1 tbsp	soya sauce	15 mL
2 tsp	sesame oil	10 mL
1 tsp	minced garlic	5 mL
1 tsp	minced ginger root	5 mL
1/2 tsp	cornstarch	2 mL

Stir-Fry

2 cups	sliced red bell peppers	500 mL
2 cups	chopped broccoli	500 mL
2 cups	snow peas	500 mL
1 cup	canned water chestnuts, drained and chopped	250 mL
1/2 cup	chopped green onions	125 mL
1/3 cup	chopped fresh coriander	75 mL

1. In a pot of boiling water, cook pasta 8 to 10 minutes or until tender but firm. Drain. In a bowl stir together pasta and sesame oil; spread over bottom of prepared pan. Bake 25 minutes. Turn oven to broil; cook another 3 to 5 minutes or until crisp and brown.

2. In a small bowl, stir together cashews, water, honey, lemon juice, soya sauce, sesame oil, garlic, ginger and cornstarch; set aside.

3. In a large nonstick wok or frying pan sprayed with vegetable spray, heat 2 tbsp (25 mL) water over high heat. Stir-fry red peppers and broccoli for 3 minutes. Add snow peas; stir-fry 1 minute. Add water chestnuts and sauce; cook 1 minute or until sauce thickens slightly. Stir in green onions and coriander.

4. Pour over pasta basket. Serve immediately.

Sweet Potato Maple Syrup Cannelloni

Preheat oven to 375° F (190° C)

13- by 9-inch (3 L) baking dish

12	cannelloni shells	12

Filling

1 3/4 cups	diced peeled sweet potatoes	425 mL
2/3 cup	5% ricotta cheese	150 mL
1/3 cup	light cream cheese, softened	75 mL
4 tsp	maple syrup	20 mL
1/2 tsp	ground cinnamon	2 mL
2 tsp	vegetable oil	10 mL
1 1/2 tsp	minced garlic	7 mL
2/3 cup	chopped red bell peppers	150 mL
1/4 cup	chopped onions	50 mL

Sauce

2 tsp	margarine *or* butter	10 mL
4 tsp	all-purpose flour	20 mL
3/4 cup	2% milk	175 mL
1/2 cup	BASIC VEGETABLE STOCK (see recipe, page 36)	125 mL
Pinch	ground nutmeg	Pinch
1 tbsp	grated Parmesan cheese	15 mL

1. In a large pot of boiling water, cook cannelloni 12 minutes or until tender. Rinse under cold water, drain and set aside.

2. In a small saucepan, add cold water to cover sweet potatoes. Bring to a boil; cook 10 to 15 minutes or until tender. Drain; transfer to food processor. Add ricotta, cream cheese, maple syrup and cinnamon; process until smooth.

3. In a nonstick frying pan, heat oil over medium-high heat. Add garlic, red peppers and onions; cook 4 minutes or until softened. Stir into sweet potato mixture.

4. Stuff each cannelloni shell with 3 tbsp (45 mL) filling. Put in baking dish.

5. Make the sauce: In a small nonstick saucepan, melt margarine over medium-low heat. Stir in flour; cook, stirring, 1 minute. Gradually whisk in milk, stock and nutmeg. Continue to cook, whisking, 3 minutes or until thickened. Pour over cannelloni. Sprinkle with Parmesan.

6. Cover dish tightly with foil. Bake 15 minutes or until heated through.

Caesar Corn and Red Pepper Risotto

SERVES 4 TO 6

TIP

You can replace the roasted red bell peppers with 4 oz (125 g) water-packed red peppers.

Try a combination of white and wild rice. Cook separately, as wild rice takes longer.

The sauce in this recipe tastes wonderful over salad.

MAKE AHEAD

Broil vegetables, prepare sauce and rice up to 2 days in advance. Combine just before serving.

Preheat oven to broil
Baking sheet

1	large red bell pepper	1
1	can (12 oz [341 mL]) corn, drained	1

Sauce

1	egg	1
1/4 cup	grated Parmesan cheese	50 mL
3 tbsp	olive oil	45 mL
1 tbsp	freshly squeezed lemon juice	15 mL
1 tbsp	red wine vinegar	15 mL
2 tsp	Dijon mustard	10 mL
1 1/2 tsp	minced garlic	7 mL

Rice

3 cups	BASIC VEGETABLE STOCK (see recipe, page 36)	750 mL
1 1/2 cups	white or brown rice	375 mL
2 tsp	vegetable oil	10 mL
1 1/2 tsp	minced garlic	7 mL
3/4 cup	chopped onions	175 mL
1/2 cup	chopped fresh parsley	125 mL

1. Arrange oven rack 6 inches (15 cm) from element. Put pepper and spread out corn on baking sheet. Cook approximately 20 minutes, stirring corn and turning pepper occasionally, or until corn and peppers are blistered and charred. (Some of the corn will pop.) When pepper is cool enough to handle, stem, seed, peel and chop.

2. Meanwhile, make the sauce: In a food processor or blender, combine egg, Parmesan, olive oil, lemon juice, vinegar, Dijon and garlic; purée until smooth. Set aside.

PER SERVING (6)

Calories	321
Protein	7 g
Fat, total	11 g
Fat, saturated	2 g
Carbohydrates	49 g
Sodium	193 mg
Cholesterol	39 mg
Fiber	2 g

3. In a saucepan bring stock to a boil; stir in rice. Cover, reduce heat to medium-low and cook 15 to 20 minutes or until rice is tender. (If using brown rice, increase cooking time to 30 minutes and add more stock if necessary.)

4. In a nonstick frying pan, heat oil over medium-high heat. Add garlic and onions; cook 4 minutes or until softened. Stir in corn and peppers; cook 2 minutes or until heated through. Stir vegetable mixture into hot cooked rice. Pour sauce over and toss to coat. Garnish with chopped parsley and serve immediately.

Tortellini with Marinara Sauce and Sun-Dried Tomatoes

TIP

This is such a versatile and delicious sauce that I decided to produce it commercially. But it's still best made from scratch.

To soften sun-dried tomatoes, pour boiling water over them and soak 15 minutes or until soft. Drain and chop.

MAKE AHEAD

Prepare sauce up to 3 days in advance. Freeze for up to 4 weeks.

1 tsp	vegetable oil	5 mL
2 tsp	minced garlic	10 mL
3/4 cup	chopped onions	175 mL
1	can (19 oz [540 mL]) tomatoes, crushed	1
1/2 cup	chopped softened sun-dried tomatoes (see Tip, at left)	125 mL
1/3 cup	sliced black olives	75 mL
2 tbsp	red or white wine	25 mL
1 tsp	dried basil	5 mL
1/2 tsp	dried oregano	2 mL
1	bay leaf	1
1 lb	frozen cheese tortellini	500 g
1 1/2 oz	feta cheese, crumbled	40 g

1. In a nonstick saucepan, heat oil over medium heat. Add garlic and onions; cook 4 minutes or until softened. Add tomatoes, sun-dried tomatoes, olives, wine, basil, oregano and bay leaf; bring to a boil, reduce heat to low and cook for 20 minutes.

2. In a large pot of boiling water, cook tortellini until tender but firm; drain and put in a serving bowl. Pour sauce over and sprinkle with feta cheese.

PER SERVING	
Calories	478
Protein	19 g
Fat, total	15 g
Fat, saturated	4 g
Carbohydrates	70 g
Sodium	1340 mg
Cholesterol	11 mg
Fiber	4 g

DESSERTS

Double Chocolate Chip Banana Cake

◆■◆■◆■◆■◆━━◆━━■◆■◆■◆■◆

SERVES 12

TIP

The surprise ingredient here is zucchini, which gives incredible moisture to the cake. If zucchini is not available, substitute carrots.

Freeze overripe bananas in their skins up to 3 months. Defrost and use mashed in baking.

Leave out the icing if you wish — but it is delicious!

MAKE AHEAD

Bake up to 2 days in advance.

Freeze tightly wrapped for up to 6 weeks.

Preheat oven to 350° F (180° C)

12-cup (3 L) Bundt pan

1 cup	packed brown sugar	250 mL
1/2 cup	granulated sugar	125 mL
1/3 cup	vegetable oil	75 mL
1	ripe medium banana, mashed	1
1 tsp	vanilla extract	5 mL
2	eggs	2
2 cups	finely chopped or grated peeled zucchini *or* carrots (about 8 oz [250 g])	500 mL
1/2 cup	canned crushed pineapple	125 mL
2 cups	all-purpose flour	500 mL
1/3 cup	cocoa	75 mL
1 1/2 tsp	baking powder	7 mL
1 1/2 tsp	baking soda	7 mL
1/3 cup	semi-sweet chocolate chips	75 mL
1/4 cup	light sour cream	50 mL

Chocolate Cream Cheese Icing

1/3 cup	light cream cheese, softened	75 mL
1 cup	icing sugar	250 mL
1 tbsp	cocoa	15 mL
1 tbsp	2% milk	15 mL

1. In a food processor, combine brown sugar, granulated sugar, oil, banana, vanilla and eggs; process until smooth. Add zucchini and pineapple; process just until combined.

2. In a bowl stir together flour, cocoa, baking powder and baking soda. Stir wet ingredients into dry ingredients just until mixed. Stir in chocolate chips and sour cream. Spoon into prepared pan. Bake 40 to 45 minutes or until tester inserted in center comes out clean. Let cool.

3. With an electric mixer, cream together cream cheese, icing sugar, cocoa and milk. Spread over cooled cake.

PER SERVING	
Calories	361
Protein	5 g
Fat, total	10 g
Fat, saturated	3.0 g
Carbohydrates	65 g
Sodium	246 mg
Cholesterol	40 mg
Fiber	3 g

CREAM CHEESE-FILLED BROWNIES (PAGE 169) ➤

Banana Chocolate Meringue Pie

◆■◆■◆■◆⬥◆■◆■◆■◆

Preheat oven to 425° F (220° C)
8-inch (2 L) springform pan sprayed with vegetable spray

Crust

1 1/2 cups	chocolate wafer crumbs	375 mL
2 tbsp	water	25 mL
1 tbsp	vegetable oil	15 mL

Filling

1 1/4 cups	2% evaporated milk	300 mL
1/2 cup	granulated sugar	125 mL
3 tbsp	cocoa	45 mL
4 tsp	cornstarch	20 mL
2	egg yolks (see Tip, at left)	2
3 tbsp	semi-sweet chocolate chips	45 mL
1 tsp	vanilla extract	5 mL
2	ripe medium bananas	2

Meringue Topping

3	egg whites	3
1/4 tsp	cream of tartar	1 mL
1/2 cup	granulated sugar	125 mL

1. Make the crust: In a bowl combine chocolate wafer crumbs, water and oil. Press mixture onto bottom and sides of prepared pan. Refrigerate.

2. Make the filling: In a saucepan heat 3/4 cup (175 mL) of the evaporated milk until hot. In a bowl whisk remaining evaporated milk, sugar, cocoa, cornstarch and egg yolks until smooth. Whisk hot milk into bowl; return mixture to saucepan and cook over medium heat, whisking, about 4 minutes or until thickened. Remove from heat. Stir in chocolate chips and vanilla until chips melt. Slice bananas and arrange over bottom of crust; pour hot filling over.

3. Make the topping: In a bowl with an electric mixer, beat egg whites with cream of tartar until soft peaks form. Gradually add sugar; continue beating until stiff peaks form. Decoratively spoon or pipe over hot filling, spreading to sides of pan. Bake until golden brown, about 8 to 10 minutes. Cool on wire rack. Chill before serving.

< SOUR CREAM ORANGE APPLE CAKE (PAGE 180)

Mocha Roll with Chocolate Fudge Filling

◆■◆■◆■◆■◆⬦◆■◆■◆■◆■◆

TIPS

Remember to use enough icing sugar on towel and cake to prevent sticking.

For a different taste, substitute chocolate liqueur for the coffee.

Roll carefully, using a tea towel to assist. Keep towel inside the roll until it cools. Be sure to remove towel before filling!

Roll may crack slightly. Don't worry; just keep rolling.

MAKE AHEAD

Prepare filling up to 2 days in advance.

Best eaten within 2 days.

PER SERVING	
Calories	300
Protein	11 g
Fat, total	5 g
Fat, saturated	3.0 g
Carbohydrates	57 g
Sodium	106 mg
Cholesterol	67 mg
Fiber	2 g

Preheat oven to 350° F (180° C)

15- by 10-inch (37.5 by 25 cm) jelly roll pan lined with parchment paper and sprayed with vegetable spray

Cake

2	egg yolks	2
1/3 cup	granulated sugar	75 mL
3 tbsp	brewed strong coffee	45 mL
1/3 cup	all-purpose flour	75 mL
1/4 cup	cocoa	50 mL
4	egg whites	4
1/4 tsp	cream of tartar	1 mL
1/2 cup	granulated sugar	125 mL
	Icing sugar	

Filling

1 cup	5% ricotta cheese	250 mL
1/2 cup	icing sugar	125 mL
3 tbsp	cocoa	45 mL
1 tbsp	brewed strong coffee	15 mL

Icing

3/4 cup	icing sugar	175 mL
1 tbsp	cocoa	15 mL
1 1/2 to 2 tbsp	hot water	20 to 25 mL

1. Make the cake: In a bowl with an electric mixer, beat egg yolks with sugar until thickened and pale; beat in coffee. Sift flour and cocoa into another bowl; add to yolk mixture, gently folding in. In a separate bowl, beat egg whites with cream of tartar until frothy; gradually add granulated sugar, beating until stiff peaks form. Stir one-quarter of the egg whites into the yolk mixture; fold in the remaining egg whites. Spoon onto prepared jelly roll pan,

spreading to edges and leveling top. Bake 15 minutes or until tester comes out clean. Cool 5 minutes. Sprinkle with a little icing sugar. Sprinkle a clean tea towel with some icing sugar. Invert cake onto towel; remove pan and gently peel away parchment paper. Sprinkle with some more icing sugar. Starting at short end, roll cake and tea towel up together. Let cool completely.

2. Meanwhile, make the filling: In a food processor, combine ricotta, icing sugar, cocoa and coffee; process until smooth.

3. Make the icing: In a bowl whisk together sugar, cocoa and hot water until smooth.

4. Assembly: Carefully unroll cake. Spread with filling. Roll up, using tea towel to help. Carefully transfer to serving platter. Spread with icing.

Pear and Raisin Custard Crumble

Preheat oven to 350° F (180° C)
9-inch (2.5 L) springform pan sprayed with vegetable spray

Crust
1 1/2 cups	graham cracker crumbs	375 mL
2 tbsp	packed brown sugar	25 mL
2 1/2 tbsp	water	35 mL
1 tbsp	vegetable oil	15 mL
1/4 tsp	ground cinnamon	1 mL

Filling
3 cups	peeled diced pears (3 large)	750 mL
1/2 cup	raisins	125 mL
3 tbsp	packed brown sugar	45 mL
1/2 tsp	ground cinnamon	2 mL

Custard
1 cup	2% evaporated milk	250 mL
1/4 cup	granulated sugar	50 mL
2 tbsp	all-purpose flour	25 mL
1 tsp	vanilla extract	5 mL
1	egg yolk	1

Topping
1/2 cup	all-purpose flour	125 mL
1/3 cup	rolled oats	75 mL
1/4 cup	packed brown sugar	50 mL
2 tbsp	margarine *or* butter	25 mL
1/2 tsp	ground cinnamon	2 mL

1. In a bowl combine graham crumbs, brown sugar, water, oil and cinnamon. Press onto bottom and sides of prepared springform pan.

2. In a bowl combine pears, raisins, brown sugar and cinnamon. In a separate bowl, whisk together milk, sugar, flour, vanilla and egg yolk until well blended. In another bowl, combine flour, oats, brown sugar, margarine and cinnamon until crumbly.

3. Spoon pear mixture into crust. Pour custard mixture over. Sprinkle evenly with topping mixture. Bake 40 minutes or until pears are tender and custard is set.

Banana Chocolate Marble Cheesecake

◆■◆■◆■◆■◆■◆ ◆◆◆ ■◆■◆■◆■◆■◆

SERVES 10 TO 12

TIP

Freeze overripe bananas in their skins up to 3 months. Defrost and use mashed in baking.

MAKE AHEAD

Bake up to 2 days in advance. Freeze for up to 6 weeks.

Preheat oven to 350° F (180° C)

8 1/2-inch (2.25 L) springform pan sprayed with vegetable spray

Crust

1 1/2 cups	chocolate wafer crumbs	375 mL
2 tbsp	water	25 mL
1 tbsp	vegetable oil	15 mL

Filling

1 1/2 cups	5% ricotta cheese	375 mL
3/4 cup	granulated sugar	175 mL
2/3 cup	light sour cream	150 mL
1/3 cup	light cream cheese	75 mL
1	medium ripe banana, mashed	1
1	egg	1
2 tbsp	all-purpose flour	25 mL
2 tsp	vanilla extract	10 mL
3 tbsp	semi-sweet chocolate chips	45 mL
1 tbsp	water	15 mL

1. Make the crust: In a bowl combine chocolate wafer crumbs, water and oil. Press mixture onto bottom and sides of prepared springform pan.

2. Make the filling: In a large bowl or in a food processor, beat together ricotta, sugar, sour cream, cream cheese, banana, egg, flour and vanilla until well blended. Pour into crust and smooth top.

3. Melt chocolate chips with water in microwave on High for 30 seconds and stir until smooth. Spoon onto cheesecake in several places; with a knife, swirl through lightly.

4. Bake 40 to 45 minutes or until set around edges but still slightly loose at center. Cool on wire rack. Chill before serving.

PER SERVING (12)	
Calories	215
Protein	8 g
Fat, total	7 g
Fat, saturated	3.0 g
Carbohydrates	30 g
Sodium	145 mg
Cholesterol	40 mg
Fiber	0 g

Banana Spice Cake with Cream Cheese Frosting

◆▢◆▢◆▢◆◀━━━━▶◆▢◆▢◆▢◆

Preheat oven to 350° F (180° C)

12-cup (3 L) Bundt pan sprayed with vegetable spray

SERVES 12

TIP

Increase amount of spices to your taste — or omit any not on hand.

Freeze overripe bananas in their skins up to 3 months. Defrost and use mashed in baking.

Use as a muffin batter. Bake 15 to 20 minutes or until tester comes out clean.

MAKE AHEAD

Bake up to 2 days in advance. Freeze for up to 6 weeks.

Cake

1/3 cup	margarine *or* butter	75 mL
3/4 cup	granulated sugar	175 mL
1/2 cup	packed brown sugar	125 mL
2	eggs	2
3/4 cup	light sour cream	175 mL
2 tsp	vanilla extract	10 mL
1	medium ripe banana, mashed	1
1 1/2 cups	all-purpose flour	375 mL
2 tsp	baking powder	10 mL
1 1/2 tsp	ground cinnamon	7 mL
1 tsp	baking soda	5 mL
1/8 tsp	ground allspice	0.5 mL
1/8 tsp	ground ginger	0.5 mL
1/8 tsp	ground nutmeg	0.5 mL

Icing

1/3 cup	light cream cheese, softened	75 mL
2/3 cup	icing sugar	150 mL
1 tbsp	2% milk	15 mL

1. Make the cake: In a food processor or in a bowl with an electric mixer, cream together margarine, sugar and brown sugar. Add eggs one at a time, beating well after each; beat in sour cream, vanilla and banana. In a separate bowl, stir together flour, baking powder, cinnamon, baking soda, allspice, ginger and nutmeg. Add liquid ingredients to dry ingredients, blending just until mixed. Pour into prepared pan.

2. Bake 35 minutes or until cake tester inserted in center comes out clean. Cool in pan on wire rack.

3. Make icing: In a bowl or food processor, beat together cream cheese, icing sugar and milk until smooth.

4. Invert cake and drizzle icing over top.

PER SERVING

Calories	250
Protein	4 g
Fat, total	6 g
Fat, saturated	2.0 g
Carbohydrates	43 g
Sodium	269 mg
Cholesterol	41 mg
Fiber	1 g

Blueberry Lemon Cornmeal Muffins

MAKES 12

TIP

Fresh blueberries are always best tasting, especially the small ones available in the summer.

If using frozen berries, do not thaw. The flour will help to absorb the excess liquid.

These muffins are great for breakfast on the run.

MAKE AHEAD

Bake up to 2 days in advance; store in an air-tight container.

Freeze for up to 6 weeks.

Preheat oven to 350° F (180° C)

12 muffin cups sprayed with vegetable spray

3/4 cup	granulated sugar	175 mL
1/4 cup	margarine *or* butter	50 mL
1	egg	1
3 tbsp	freshly squeezed lemon juice	45 mL
3 tbsp	2% milk	45 mL
1 1/2 tsp	grated lemon zest	7 mL
1 cup	all-purpose flour	250 mL
1/4 cup	cornmeal	50 mL
1 1/2 tsp	baking powder	7 mL
1 tsp	baking soda	5 mL
1/2 cup	2% plain yogurt	125 mL
1 1/4 cups	fresh or frozen blueberries	300 mL
2 tsp	all-purpose flour	10 mL

1. In a large bowl with an electric mixer, beat sugar, margarine, egg, lemon juice, milk and lemon zest until well blended. (Mixture may appear curdled.)

2. In another bowl, stir together flour, cornmeal, baking powder and baking soda. Add flour mixture and yogurt alternately to creamed mixture. In a small bowl, toss blueberries with flour; fold into batter. Divide batter among muffin cups.

3. Bake 20 to 25 minutes or until tops are firm to the touch and tester inserted in center comes out clean.

PER MUFFIN

Calories	149
Protein	3 g
Fat, total	4 g
Fat, saturated	1.0 g
Carbohydrates	26 g
Sodium	189 mg
Cholesterol	19 mg
Fiber	1 g

Chocolate Espresso Cake

SERVES 10 TO 12

TIP

To make cutting easier, dip knife in hot water before slicing.

For a chocolate liqueur flavor, try using half coffee and half chocolate liqueur.

This cake seems so dense and rich you'll never believe it is light. A small piece goes a long way.

Decorate with fresh berries and serve with a puréed berry sauce.

MAKE AHEAD

Prepare up to 2 days in advance or freeze up to 6 weeks.

Preheat oven to 350° F (180° C)
8-inch (2 L) springform pan sprayed with vegetable spray

1/2 cup	semi-sweet chocolate chips	125 mL
1/4 cup	espresso or strong brewed coffee	50 mL
2	eggs, separated	2
3/4 cup	granulated sugar	175 mL
3/4 cup	2% evaporated milk	175 mL
1/2 cup	cocoa	125 mL
3 tbsp	all-purpose flour	45 mL
1 tsp	vanilla extract	5 mL
3 tbsp	granulated sugar	45 mL

1. Melt chocolate chips with coffee; stir until smooth. Allow to cool.

2. In a large bowl, beat together egg yolks, 3/4 cup (175 mL) sugar, evaporated milk, cocoa, flour and vanilla until smooth. Beat in chocolate-coffee mixture.

3. With an electric mixer in a separate bowl, beat egg whites until soft peaks form. Gradually add 3 tbsp (45 mL) sugar and continue beating until stiff peaks form.

4. Stir one-quarter of egg whites into chocolate batter. Gently fold in remaining egg whites. Spoon into prepared pan. Bake 30 to 35 minutes or until cake is set at the center. Chill before serving.

PER SERVING (12)

Calories	136
Protein	3 g
Fat, total	4 g
Fat, saturated	2.0 g
Carbohydrates	24 g
Sodium	29 mg
Cholesterol	37 mg
Fiber	2 g

Cream Cheese-Filled Brownies

◆■□■◆■□■◆■◀━━▶■◆■□■◆■□■◆

Preheat oven to 350° F (180° C)
8-inch (2 L) square baking dish sprayed with vegetable spray

Filling

4 oz	light cream cheese, softened	125 g
2 tbsp	granulated sugar	25 mL
2 tbsp	2% milk	25 mL
1 tsp	vanilla extract	5 mL

Cake

1 cup	packed brown sugar	250 mL
1/3 cup	light sour cream	75 mL
1/4 cup	vegetable oil	50 mL
1	egg	1
1	egg white	1
3/4 cup	all-purpose flour	175 mL
1/2 cup	cocoa	125 mL
1 tsp	baking powder	5 mL

1. Make the filling: In a food processor or in a bowl with an electric mixer, beat together cream cheese, sugar, milk and vanilla until smooth. Set aside.

2. Make the cake: In a large bowl whisk together brown sugar, sour cream, oil, whole egg and egg white. In a separate bowl, stir together flour, cocoa and baking powder. Add liquid ingredients to dry, blending just until mixed.

3. Pour half the cake batter into prepared pan. Spoon filling on top; spread with a wet knife. Pour remaining batter into pan. Bake 20 to 25 minutes or until just barely loose at center.

Creamy Pumpkin Cheese Pie

SERVES 12

TIP

In the fall use fresh pumpkin. Bake pumpkin or squash in a 400° F (200° C) oven until tender, approximately 1 hour.

The topping is simple but highly decorative.

MAKE AHEAD

Bake up to 2 days in advance. Freeze up to 6 weeks.

Preheat oven to 350° F (180° C)
9-inch (2.5 L) springform pan *or* 9-inch (23 cm) deep dish pie plate

1 1/2 cups	graham cracker crumbs	375 mL
2 tbsp	granulated sugar	25 mL
2 tbsp	water	25 mL
1 tbsp	vegetable oil	15 mL
4 oz	light cream cheese	125 g
1/2 cup	5% ricotta cheese	125 mL
1/3 cup	granulated sugar	75 mL
1	egg	1
1 tsp	vanilla extract	5 mL
1 cup	canned pumpkin *or* mashed cooked butternut squash	250 mL
2/3 cup	2% evaporated milk	150 mL
3/4 cup	packed brown sugar	175 mL
1 tsp	ground cinnamon	5 mL
1/4 tsp	ground ginger	1 mL
1/4 tsp	ground nutmeg	1 mL
3 tbsp	light sour cream	45 mL
2 1/2 tsp	granulated sugar	12 mL

1. In a bowl combine graham crumbs, sugar, water and oil; press into bottom and sides of pan; set aside.
2. In a food processor, combine cream cheese, ricotta, sugar, egg and vanilla; process until smooth. Pour into prepared crust.
3. In a food processor, combine pumpkin, evaporated milk, sugar, cinnamon, ginger and nutmeg until well blended. Spoon carefully over cheese filling.
4. In a small bowl, stir together sour cream and sugar. Put in a squeeze bottle or in a small plastic sandwich bag with the very tip of corner cut off. Draw 4 concentric circles on top of pumpkin filling. Run a toothpick through the circles at regular intervals.
5. Bake 50 minutes or until just slightly loose at the center. Cool on wire rack. Chill before serving

PER SERVING

Calories	203
Protein	6 g
Fat, total	5 g
Fat, saturated	2.0 g
Carbohydrates	34 g
Sodium	209 mg
Cholesterol	29 mg
Fiber	1 g

Date Roll-Up Cookies

Preheat oven to 350° F (180° C)
Large baking sheet sprayed with vegetable spray

Filling

8 oz	pitted dried dates	250 g
1 cup	orange juice	250 mL
1/4 tsp	ground cinnamon	1 mL

Dough

2 1/4 cups	all-purpose flour	550 mL
2/3 cup	granulated sugar	150 mL
1/4 cup	margarine *or* butter	50 mL
1/4 cup	vegetable oil	50 mL
1/4 cup	2% plain yogurt	50 mL
3 tbsp	water	45 mL
1 tsp	vanilla extract	5 mL
1 tsp	grated orange zest	5 mL

1. Make the filling: In a saucepan bring dates, orange juice and cinnamon to a boil; reduce heat to medium-low and cook 10 minutes or until soft. Mash with a fork until liquid is absorbed. Refrigerate.

2. Make the dough: In a food processor, combine flour, sugar, margarine, oil, yogurt, water, vanilla and orange zest; process until dough forms. Add up to 1 tbsp (15 mL) more water, if necessary. Divide dough in half; form each half into a ball, wrap and refrigerate for 15 minutes or until chilled.

3. Between 2 sheets of waxed paper sprinkled with flour, roll one of the dough balls into a rectangle, approximately 12 by 10 inches (30 by 25 cm) and 1/8 inch (5 mm) thick. Remove top sheet of waxed paper. Spread half of date mixture over rolled dough. Starting at short end and using the waxed paper as an aid, roll up tightly. Cut into 1/2-inch (1 cm) slices and place on prepared baking sheet. Repeat with remaining dough and filling.

4. Bake 25 minutes or until lightly browned.

Gingerbread Biscotti

MAKES 40 TO 48

TIP

To increase fiber, use 2/3 cup (150 mL) whole wheat flour and 1 2/3 cups (400 mL) all-purpose flour.

Increase, decrease or omit spices, according to your personal taste.

For a decadent treat, melt 2 oz (50 g) semi-sweet chocolate and dip ends of cookies. Let harden.

MAKE AHEAD

Bake up to 1 week in advance, keeping in air-tight containers. Freeze for up to 6 weeks.

Preheat oven to 350° F (180° C)

Baking sheet sprayed with vegetable spray

3/4 cup	packed brown sugar	175 mL
1/4 cup	margarine *or* butter	50 mL
1/4 cup	molasses	50 mL
2	eggs	2
1 tsp	vanilla extract	5 mL
2 1/3 cups	all-purpose flour	575 mL
2 1/4 tsp	baking powder	11 mL
1 tsp	ground cinnamon	5 mL
1 tsp	ground ginger	5 mL
1/2 tsp	ground allspice	2 mL
1/4 tsp	ground nutmeg	1 mL

1. In a food processor or in a bowl with an electric mixer, beat together brown sugar, margarine, molasses, eggs and vanilla until smooth. In a separate bowl, stir together flour, baking powder, cinnamon, ginger, allspice and nutmeg. Add wet ingredients to dry ingredients, mixing just until combined.

2. Divide dough in half. Form each half into a log 12 inches (30 cm) long and 2 inches (5 cm) around; transfer to prepared baking sheet. Bake 20 minutes. Cool 10 minutes.

3. Cut logs on an angle into 1/2-inch (1 cm) slices. Bake 20 minutes or until lightly browned.

PER SERVING (48)	
Calories	207
Protein	1 g
Fat, total	1 g
Fat, saturated	0.2 g
Carbohydrates	9 g
Sodium	27 mg
Cholesterol	9 mg
Fiber	0 g

Four-Spice Cake with Cream Cheese Icing

◆■□■□◆□■◆■□◆◆■◆□■□◆■◆

Preheat oven to 350° F (180° C)

9-inch (2.5 L) square baking dish

1/3 cup	margarine *or* soft butter	75 mL
2/3 cup	granulated sugar	150 mL
2	eggs	2
1/3 cup	molasses	75 mL
1 tsp	vanilla extract	5 mL
1 1/2 cups	all-purpose flour	375 mL
1 tsp	baking powder	5 mL
1 tsp	ground cinnamon	5 mL
1 tsp	ground ginger	5 mL
1/2 tsp	ground allspice	2 mL
1/2 tsp	baking soda	2 mL
1/4 tsp	ground nutmeg	1 mL
1 cup	2% plain yogurt	250 mL

Cream Cheese Frosting

1/3 cup	light cream cheese	75 mL
1/2 cup	icing sugar	125 mL
1 tsp	molasses	5 mL

1. In food processor or in a bowl with an electric mixer, cream margarine with sugar. Beat in eggs one at a time. Beat in molasses and vanilla.

2. In a separate bowl, stir together flour, baking powder, cinnamon, ginger, allspice, baking soda and nutmeg until well mixed. Alternately add flour mixture and yogurt to molasses mixture. Spoon into prepared pan.

3. Bake 35 to 40 minutes or until tester inserted in center comes out clean. Cool on wire rack.

4. Make the frosting: In a food processor or in a bowl with an electric mixer, beat cream cheese, icing sugar and molasses until smooth. Spread over cake.

Lemon and Lime Poppy Seed Biscotti

TIP

If desired, omit lime and use double the quantity of lemon juice and zest.

If dough is sticky when forming into logs, try wetting your fingers.

MAKE AHEAD

Store cookies in air-tight containers for up to 1 week.

Freeze in air-tight containers up to 6 weeks.

Preheat oven to 350° F (180° C)

Baking sheet sprayed with vegetable spray

1 cup	granulated sugar	250 mL
1/4 cup	margarine *or* butter	50 mL
2	eggs	2
1 1/2 tsp	grated lime zest	7 mL
1 1/2 tsp	grated lemon zest	7 mL
2 tbsp	freshly squeezed lime juice	25 mL
2 tbsp	freshly squeezed lemon juice	25 mL
1 tsp	vanilla extract	5 mL
2 1/2 cups	all-purpose flour	625 mL
2 1/4 tsp	baking powder	11 mL
2 tsp	poppy seeds	10 mL

1. In a food processor or in a bowl with an electric mixer, beat sugar, margarine and eggs until smooth. Beat in lime zest, lemon zest, lime juice, lemon juice and vanilla.

2. In a separate bowl, stir together flour, baking powder and poppy seeds. Add wet ingredients to dry ingredients, mixing just until combined. Dough will be stiff.

3. Divide dough in half. Form each half into a log 12 inches (30 cm) long and 1 1/2 inches (4 cm) around; transfer to prepared baking sheet. Bake 20 minutes. Cool 10 minutes.

4. Cut logs on an angle into 1/2-inch (1 cm) slices. Bake 20 minutes.

PER COOKIE (40)

Calories	61
Protein	1 g
Fat, total	1 g
Fat, saturated	0.2 g
Carbohydrates	12 g
Sodium	28 mg
Cholesterol	0 mg
Fiber	0 g

Lemon Poppy Seed Squares

TIP

Here's an updated version of the comfort food classic, lemon squares — but with much less fat and calories.

Try substituting lime juice and zest for the lemon.

MAKE AHEAD

Prepare up to 2 days in advance.

Preheat oven to 350° F (180° C)
8-inch square (2 L) baking pan sprayed with vegetable spray

Cake

1/2 cup	granulated sugar	125 mL
1 tbsp	margarine *or* butter	15 mL
2 tsp	poppy seeds	10 mL
1 1/2 tsp	grated lemon zest	7 mL
1	egg	1
3/4 cup	cake and pastry flour	175 mL

Topping

2/3 cup	granulated sugar	150 mL
2 tsp	grated lemon zest	10 mL
1/3 cup	freshly squeezed lemon juice	75 mL
1 tbsp	cornstarch	15 mL
1	egg	1
1	egg white	1

1. Make the cake: In a bowl whisk together sugar, margarine, poppy seeds, lemon zest and egg until smooth. Add wet ingredients to flour and stir just until mixed. Pat into prepared pan; set aside.

2. Make the topping: In a bowl stir together sugar, lemon zest, lemon juice, cornstarch, whole egg and egg white. Pour over cake batter in pan.

3. Bake 20 to 25 minutes or until set with center still slightly soft. Cool to room temperature on a wire rack.

PER SQUARE

Calories	96
Protein	2 g
Fat, total	2 g
Fat, saturated	0.3 g
Carbohydrates	19 g
Sodium	21 mg
Cholesterol	27 mg
Fiber	0 g

Orange Cappuccino Pudding Cake

TIP

Use a flavored coffee mix powder, like Irish cream or vanilla, or a cappuccino mix.

Pudding cakes are fantastic because they give you the added bonus of a low-fat sauce.

Serve with a scoop of frozen yogurt.

MAKE AHEAD

Best served right out of the oven. But can be reheated in microwave for similar texture.

Preheat oven to 350° F (180° C)

8-inch square (2 L) baking dish sprayed with vegetable spray

1 cup	all-purpose flour	250 mL
1 cup	packed brown sugar	250 mL
2 tsp	baking powder	10 mL
2 tsp	grated orange zest	10 mL
1/2 cup	orange juice	125 mL
2 tbsp	vegetable oil	25 mL
1	egg	1
2 tsp	vanilla extract	10 mL
1/4 cup	semi-sweet chocolate chips	50 mL
1/3 cup	granulated sugar	75 mL
1/4 cup	instant coffee mix powder *or* hot chocolate mix	50 mL
1/4 cup	cocoa	50 mL

1. In a bowl stir together flour, brown sugar and baking powder. In a separate bowl, whisk together orange zest, orange juice, oil, egg and vanilla. Add the wet ingredients to the dry, blending just until mixed. Batter will be thick. Pour into prepared pan. Sprinkle chocolate chips over top.

2. In a bowl whisk together 1 1/4 cups (300 mL) hot water, sugar, coffee mix and cocoa. Pour carefully over cake batter. Bake 35 minutes or until cake springs back when touched lightly in center. Serve warm; spoon cake and underlying sauce into individual dessert dishes.

PER SERVING (10)

Calories	210
Protein	3 g
Fat, total	5 g
Fat, saturated	1.0 g
Carbohydrates	40 g
Sodium	82 mg
Cholesterol	22 mg
Fiber	2 g

Two-Tone Chocolate Orange Biscotti

MAKES 40 TO 48

TIPS

If dough is sticky when forming into logs, try wetting your fingers.

Two colors of dough make these cookies very attractive.

MAKE AHEAD

Freeze in containers for up to 6 weeks.

Preheat oven to 350° F (180° C)
Baking sheet sprayed with vegetable spray

1 1/4 cups	granulated sugar	300 mL
1/3 cup	margarine *or* butter	75 mL
2	eggs	2
2 tbsp	orange juice concentrate	25 mL
1 tbsp	grated orange zest	15 mL
2 2/3 cups	all-purpose flour	650 mL
2 1/2 tsp	baking powder	12 mL
3 tbsp	cocoa	45 mL

1. In a food processor or in a bowl with an electric mixer, beat together sugar, margarine, eggs, orange juice concentrate and orange zest until smooth. Add flour and baking powder; mix just until combined.

2. Divide dough in half; to one half, add cocoa and mix well. Divide chocolate and plain doughs in half to produce 4 doughs. Roll each piece into a long thin rope approximately 12 inches (30 cm) long and 1 inch (2.5 cm) wide. Use extra flour if too sticky. Place 1 cocoa dough on top of (or beside) each plain dough. (Ensure the plain and cocoa doughs touch one another.)

3. Bake 20 minutes. Cool 10 minutes. Cut logs on an angle into 1/2-inch (1 cm) slices. Bake another 20 minutes.

PER SERVING (48)

Calories	72
Protein	1 g
Fat, total	2 g
Fat, saturated	0.4 g
Carbohydrates	13 g
Sodium	42 mg
Cholesterol	11 mg
Fiber	0 g

Sour Cream Brownie Cheesecake

◆■◆■◆■◆◀▬▶■◆■◆■◆■◆

Preheat oven to 350° F (180° C)

8 1/2-inch (2.25 L) springform pan sprayed with vegetable spray

SERVES 12

TIP

This is my favorite decadent-but-light dessert. Children love it as much as adults do.

For a mocha-flavored brownie base, add 1 tsp (5 mL) powdered coffee, or to taste.

MAKE AHEAD

Prepare up to 1 day in advance.

Freeze tightly wrapped for up to 2 weeks.

PER SERVING

Calories	225
Protein	7 g
Fat, total	8 g
Fat, saturated	3.0 g
Carbohydrates	31 g
Sodium	122 mg
Cholesterol	47 mg
Fiber	1 g

Brownie Layer

2/3 cup	granulated sugar	150 mL
1/4 cup	vegetable oil	50 mL
1	egg	1
1 tsp	vanilla extract	5 mL
1/3 cup	all-purpose flour	75 mL
1/3 cup	cocoa	75 mL
1 tsp	baking powder	5 mL
1/4 cup	light sour cream	50 mL

Cheesecake Layer

1 cup	5% ricotta cheese	250 mL
1/2 cup	granulated sugar	125 mL
1/3 cup	light cream cheese	75 mL
1/4 cup	light sour cream	50 mL
1	egg	1
2 tbsp	all-purpose flour	25 mL
1 tsp	vanilla extract	5 mL
2 tbsp	semi-sweet chocolate chips	25 mL

Topping

1 cup	light sour cream	250 mL
2 tbsp	granulated sugar	25 mL
1 tsp	vanilla extract	5 mL
1 tbsp	semi-sweet chocolate chips	15 mL

1. Make the brownie layer: In a bowl, beat together sugar, oil, egg and vanilla. In another bowl, stir together flour, cocoa and baking powder. Stir wet mixture into dry mixture just until combined. Stir in sour cream. Pour into prepared pan.

2. Make the cheesecake layer: In a food processor, combine ricotta, sugar, cream cheese, sour cream, egg, flour and vanilla; process until smooth. Stir in chocolate chips. Pour into pan on top of brownie layer. Bake 40 minutes. Brownie batter may rise slightly over cheesecake.

3. Meanwhile, make the topping: In a small bowl, stir together sour cream, sugar and vanilla. Carefully pour over cake, smoothing with back of spoon, and sprinkle with chocolate chips. Bake 10 more minutes. Cool on a wire rack. Chill before serving.

Sour Cream Orange Apple Cake

TIP

Try chopped pears or peaches instead of apples.

To increase fiber, use 2/3 cup (150 mL) whole-wheat and 1 cup (250 mL) all-purpose flour.

Makes two 9- by 5-inch (2 L) loaves. Bake approximately 35 minutes or until tester comes out clean.

If you don't want to layer the cake, just mix apples with batter, then add topping.

MAKE AHEAD

Prepare up to 2 days in advance.

Freeze up to 6 weeks.

PER SERVING

Calories	284
Protein	4 g
Fat, total	9 g
Fat, saturated	1.0 g
Carbohydrates	49 g
Sodium	187 mg
Cholesterol	36 mg
Fiber	2 g

Preheat oven to 350° F (180° C)
10-inch (3 L) springform pan sprayed with vegetable spray

Topping

1/3 cup	packed brown sugar	75 mL
3 tbsp	chopped pecans	45 mL
1 1/2 tbsp	all-purpose flour	20 mL
2 tsp	margarine *or* butter	10 mL
1/2 tsp	ground cinnamon	2 mL

Filling

2 cups	chopped peeled apples	500 mL
1/2 cup	raisins	125 mL
1 tbsp	granulated sugar	15 mL
1 tsp	ground cinnamon	5 mL

Cake

2/3 cup	packed brown sugar	150 mL
1/2 cup	granulated sugar	125 mL
1/3 cup	vegetable oil	75 mL
2	eggs	2
1 tbsp	grated orange zest	15 mL
2 tsp	vanilla extract	10 mL
1 2/3 cups	all-purpose flour	400 mL
2 tsp	baking powder	10 mL
1 tsp	baking soda	5 mL
1/2 cup	orange juice	125 mL
1/2 cup	light sour cream	125 mL

1. Make the topping: In a small bowl, combine brown sugar, pecans, flour, margarine and cinnamon. Set aside.

2. Make the filling: In a bowl mix together apples, raisins, sugar and cinnamon. Set aside.

3. Make the cake: In a food processor or in a large bowl with an electric mixer, beat together brown sugar, granulated sugar and oil. Add eggs, one at a time, beating well after each. Mix in orange zest and vanilla.

4. In a separate bowl, stir together flour, baking powder and baking soda. In another bowl, stir together orange juice and sour cream. Add flour mixture and sour cream mixture alternately to beaten sugar mixture, mixing just until blended. Spoon half of batter into prepared pan. Top with half of apple mixture. Spoon remaining batter into pan. Top with remaining apple mixture; sprinkle with topping.

5. Bake 45 to 50 minutes, or until cake tester inserted in center comes out clean. Cool on a wire rack.

Molasses and Cinnamon Cheesecake

◆■◆■◆■◆■◀━━━▶■◆■◆■◆■◆

Preheat oven to 350° F (180° C)
8-inch (2 L) springform pan sprayed with vegetable spray

SERVES 12

TIP

Substitute other cookie crumbs for graham. Buy cookies in bulk food department and grind into crumbs.

A beautiful sour cream web design can be added just before baking. (See CREAMY PUMPKIN CHEESE PIE, page 170.)

MAKE AHEAD

Bake up to 2 days in advance.

Freeze tightly wrapped up to 6 weeks.

PER SERVING

Calories	245
Protein	9 g
Fat, total	6 g
Fat, saturated	3.0 g
Carbohydrates	39 g
Sodium	314 mg
Cholesterol	49 mg
Fiber	1 g

Crust

1 1/2 cups	graham cracker crumbs	375 mL
2 tbsp	packed brown sugar	25 mL
2 tbsp	water	25 mL
1 tbsp	vegetable oil	15 mL
1/2 tsp	ground cinnamon	2 mL

Filling

1 1/2 cups	extra-smooth 5% ricotta cheese	375 mL
1/2 cup	packed brown sugar	125 mL
1/3 cup	light cream cheese	75 mL
1/3 cup	light sour cream	75 mL
2	eggs, separated	2
2 tbsp	molasses	25 mL
2 tbsp	all-purpose flour	25 mL
1 tsp	ground cinnamon	5 mL
1 tsp	vanilla extract	5 mL
1/2 tsp	ground ginger	2 mL
1/4 tsp	ground nutmeg	1 mL
1/8 tsp	ground allspice	0.5 mL
2 tbsp	granulated sugar	25 mL

1. Make the crust: In a bowl stir together graham crumbs, brown sugar, water, oil and cinnamon. Pat mixture onto bottom and sides of prepared springform pan.

2. Make the filling: In a food processor or in a bowl, beat together ricotta, brown sugar, cream cheese, sour cream, egg yolks, molasses, flour, cinnamon, vanilla, ginger, nutmeg and allspice until smooth. In a separate bowl, beat egg whites until foamy; gradually add sugar, beating until stiff peaks form; fold into batter. Pour into crust.

3. Bake 45 to 50 minutes or until slightly loose just at center. Cool on wire rack. Chill before serving.

INDEX